I would love to acknowledge the following Angels for their generous love and support of this project.

My heartfelt thanks to:

Hal Zina Bennett
Bonnie Block
Patricia Chambers
Herb Cheifetz
Rita Cheifetz
Jack DeRosa
Donna and Magued Duncan-Nawar
Gwen Gibson
Hansine Goran
Mary Ann Maggiore
Connie Parsons
Scott Pederson
Michele Phillips
David Sherman
Susan Sparrow
Lauren Teger
Susan Tyler
Susan Zerner

A Sense of Delight

A SENSE OF DELIGHT

*Living ordinary life
in an extraordinary way!
by
Nance Cheifetz*

Ruby Shoes Press

Ruby Shoes Press
454 Las Gallinas
Suite 333
San Rafael, CA 94903
(415) 499-9161

First Edition

Printed in the United States of America

This book goes extremely well with cookies!

Acknowledgements

With Immense Love to the following people:

My heartfelt thanks to Hansine'SinaBean'Goran who appeared as a brilliant angel in my life and has been working overtime since, hovering around overhead and in my fax machine. There is no way to express my gratitude for her generosity, love, faith, inspiration and for always pointing me back to God.

To Linda Cordova for her friendship and for hanging in with me throughout this project (ok, so I was a year off in my calculations!). Thank you for your great humor, positive can-do attitude, and the fabulous job you do with everything, particularly typing out this whole manuscript.

To Jack DeRosa for his encouragement, faith, and unshakable belief in me and in this book. Everyone could use a friend who tells them when they are freaking out, "Nothing that a good night's sleep, and a pizza wouldn't fix." (See, I am not a fictional character.)

To Susan Sparrow for her loving energy, sage advice, and unbelievable gift of help in putting this book together. Clarence, give her her wings!

To Hal Zina Bennett for sharing his expertise and gift of knowledge. Read his books, they are wonderful!

To Paul Seelig, an editing (and otherwise) angel that appeared out of thin air and landed on my doorstep one day. I love it when that happens.

To P.J. Mathis for her daily "You keep going girl" calls and transformative hikes.

To Annie Servedio for her gentle spirit, enduring friendship and editing help.

To Brian Donahue for being such a great playmate and the inspiration for so many adventures (How's that for a dating endorsement!).

To Jay Levinson for his generosity, enthusiasm and help. How many people do you know (famous ones at that!) who start off their conversation with you by saying "I've got all the time in the world for you."

To Amanita Rosenbush for making me look a lot deeper than I had planned to, and for her great assistance.

To Susan Page for my first note of encouragement which I kept on my wall as a reminder.

To Mona Breed for driving me around dressed up as an angel and taking such fun photographs.

To Charles Goran for his wizardly expertise on the cover art.

To Jeanette Vonier at Elegant Images for her photographs and helping me learn how to fly (you don't want to know!).

Thank you to my terrific family. To my mom Rita Beit Cheifetz for recognizing my character traits at such an early age and naming me "Eloise" (although I'm not sure it was meant as a compliment) and for loving me and holding me in your heart all through my life. Also for keeping me supplied with chocolate ...no easy task. To Herb Cheifetz, my Dad, great heart friend and avid supporter. (Dad, if we hadn't gone skiing during my typing class in high school, I might have been able to type this manuscript. Incidentally, we made the right choice.) You both finally get to see my antics in print. To my sister, Barbara , who is probably one of the funniest people I've ever met, who kept me howling through some very difficult times. If you ever get sick in Plantation, Florida, look her up...she's a nurse. To my brother, Jonathan, who is probably one of the nicest people I've met.

To Oscar 'Rusty' Skowron for always believing in me, especially during a time when he pretty much had the field to himself.

To my great assortment of brave, loving and inspiring friends who've cheered me on (in no particular order)   Aida Devalle, Connie Parsons, Gwen Gibson, Annie Richardson, Donna Duncan,

Joni Avrutick, Donna Peters, Carolyn Smith, Michael Levine, Susan Zerner, P.J. Mathis, Brian O'Reilly, Paula Seelig, Phil Servedio, Patricia Chambers, Tree McIntyre Bader, Tracy Ginsberg and Lynn Ryder.

To Jack Canfield for his kindness in taking the time to respond to me.

To the folks that I shared the FSS Workshop with this past summer, who so generously responded to me with support and encouragement.

To my impossibly beautiful and talented resident playmates Jamie Elisabeth and Jessie Laurel who have laughed with me, rooted me on, held the faith when I temporarily misplaced mine and have participated in every crazy idea I've ever had without blinking an eye. (Ok, maybe once or twice, but you would have too!) Girls, you are an amazing gift in my life. Always remember that everything is indeed possible, and you go for it!

To John Sievert, David Cook and the folks at the Bay Area Independent Publishers Association for their great assistance and desire to help everyone succeed.

To all the others who have contributed to me on my journey, I say a silent prayer of thanks. There is a wonderful quote that pretty much sums up my feeling of gratitude to all of you...

> *You have not lived a perfect day, even though you have earned your money unless you have done something for someone who will never be able to repay you.*
>
> RUTH SMELZER

Ain't that the truth?

Hey Dad, we made it!

Contents

Section Three
Follow the Yellow Brick Road
Great adventures

Section Four
Stoking the Flames...
Evenings for lovers

Section Five
Got Joy?

Section Six
Summing Up

Dedicated to
the full expression
of our true nature
which is only love

Let's say you woke up one day...

and found your own personal Fairy
Godmother standing by the foot of your
bed. She wasn't your typical turn-
pumpkins-into-coaches variety, or mice-
into-horses (so your pets were safe for
the moment!) but she came in response
to a call to bring more delight into your
life and to awaken your heart to
playfulness and love in a way it hadn't
been open to for a very long time....

Section

One

Opening the Door to Joy

If someone were to wave a magic wand and ask what we wished for in our lives, the answer, in some form or another, would probably be more happiness, joy and delight. What that might look like would be different for each of us. For some it might be opening to more spontaneity  and humor. For others it might mean access to a more childlike, playful self. Delight might take the form of a deepening appreciation and intimacy with a partner, friend or child. Or it might be expressed in the way you approach an exciting work project or your pursuit of passionate interests. If you were asked if you are creating all the delight you want and are capable of in life, how would you answer? Is your life a demonstration of the best that you are capable of giving and receiving? Do you take the time to deepen and strengthen relationships with those you love? If you were offered the opportunity, the skills and the know-how, would you choose to spend more time on what nourishes your heart and soul?

I don't know about you but when I go looking for a book about transforming situations through delight, celebration and playfulness, I've come up empty-handed. There are self help books on endless topics, usually accompanied by numerous (and I do mean numerous) enclosed exercises to shift your belief system. There are marriage-saving books that you pick up with a groan in a last ditch effort to solve communication difficulties. There are books to inspire romance and enhance libido, such as *Creative Sexual Mastery in 5 Minutes a Day*, and *65 Orgasms in 65 Seconds - What's taking you so long*? There are healing books and cookbooks on

3

everything from *Tofu as a Path to Enlightenment* to *Better Health Through Better Lattes*. Then there are the party/celebration books for yourself and the kids in your life. You know the type: *300 Exotic Things to do with Napkins*; *250 Ways to Entertain your Toddler with Spaghetti*; and *Home Decorating Party tips for under $1.00*. (Don't miss *Ornamental Broccoli Centerpieces*.) I always end up feeling like the village idiot when I am done, especially if the books contain photos of the way it's supposed to look. (You make a jacket for your pet parakeet out of napkins!) These books are aiming to enhance the quality of health and joy in life, and they do that within their limits, but for me they only skim the surface. They don't touch the real depth of what joy and celebration are really about.

What do I mean when I talk about delight and celebration? Delight is life's wonderful healing elixir. Joy and laughter are life's secret ingredients and everyone wants the formulas for them. After all, it is through these that we somehow learn to marry our spirit, our talents, our creativity and our passion.

Delight opens our eyes and deepens our faith in ourselves, each other and life. It is nearly impossible to feel anxious and fearful when you are feeling delighted and joyful. I look at it as stepping into the UP elevator on our way to experiencing our true and boundless greater self. When you are feeling full of delight, you are capable of much greater leaps, because in those moments you are more open to possibility and are not holding onto limitation, blame or anger. This leaves space for miraculous shifts to occur.

Delight makes a difference. Humor softens even the hardest of hearts, and vulnerability, when placed tenderly in the most trusting of places, flowers in beautiful ways. Inviting love into your life and putting your energy into places where it will flourish, enhances every aspect of your being. These changes then come about not through toothgrinding force of will, but through getting out of our own way and letting love, creativity and possibility ignite the spirit of change.

4

I think I have always recognized the importance of joy in life. When I was in college, I remember laying on the lawn one spring day, and having one of my professors ask me what I wanted to do as a career when I grew up. I answered, "I want to be a Magician or a Fairy Godmother. I want to help people feel magic and possibility in life."

I came to my work early in life. My mother nicknamed me Eloise, after that hilarious character created by Kay Thompson, who lived at the Park Plaza in New York City, and drove the place wild with her antics. She had a vibrant and irrepressible spirit, as well as a turtle who ordered raisins from room service. When I set the table, I would make it into a Mad Hatter's Tea Party, with all the clocks set at 13 o'clock (a clever trick). Dinners became adventures in foreign countries. Parties were costume affairs and ordinary celebrations became carnivals. I was known to save Daylight Savings time, and put the hour away to use as I pleased (not at 2:00 a.m., thank you, when I am fast asleep). I would pull it out like a treasure on Monday mornings and relish every moment of it.

Throughout adolescence and into college, I volunteered and set up programs for senior citizens, kid's groups, and the schools. I always brought a unique perspective to them, and began to feel how responsive people became. Delight and joy, besides being fun, makes a huge difference in relationships.

My first job after graduate school was a challenging one at a Nursing Rehab Center with elderly wheelchair-bound patients. I was hired to be part of the interdisciplinary team (code: paperwork drone) and Recreational Therapist. Until then, things had been handled in a pretty conventional, by-the-book fashion. I became a detective; in my encounters, I was looking for a way to connect with patients in a meaningful fashion. What did they love? What did they value? What was missing that I could provide? How could I use what they told me to be truly helpful?

5

In such a depressing medical environment, could delight, creativity and surprise expand boundaries and possibilities? Would it inspire interest, hope or curiosity for people who had little will to live? People felt isolated and lonely. Their days were predictable, redundant and without spontaneity or hope for change. I began to turn the institutional setting upside down. I created circuses where we all dressed up and I was the two-headed master of ceremonies. (My assistant and I actually squeezed into one outfit and would walk around tethered to each other for the day. It was a very large pair of pants!) I contracted with the local zoo to bring in as many kinds of animals as they could for the residents to touch and cuddle. I created spirit days, dance classes, and dressed up as an assortment of characters, and could be seen on occasion as a bunny rabbit hopping down the hospital green hallways. I brought in every kind of performance artist I could round up. People who had been completely unresponsive started coming out of their rooms on their own. Before they showed up at events they had groomed themselves. Now that they had something fun and interesting to look forward to, their agitation levels went down and for some their medications were decreased. I noticed that some staff members were really enjoying the transformation and were delighted by their patients' responsiveness. There were others who were intimidated by the changes as the residents began to speak up more and express their preferences.

Some staff members struggled against the change since it disrupted the rigid patterns of care which they believed made their jobs easier. I learned a lot of important lessons from that experience. In even the most restrictive settings, awakening a mood of celebration and delight, with a touch of magic, brightened nearly everyone's life. I realized that there is a place of delight in all of us, just waiting to be revealed. It is present even when we cannot feel any conscious desire to go there. Eventually I found the institutional setting much too restrictive and decided to move on. As my last act, I was stopped by the Administrator when I tried to bring in a horse and hay for rides around the courtyard. (Ok, time to move on. I can take a hint!)

I moved out of social services and decided to try my hand at business. Where could I go with my skills? (Not too many calls in business for a person who wears two heads well!) I really had no intention to go into sales, but one rainy day, I was reading the classifieds and found an ad for a company who wanted someone to sell rainbows. It had my name on it - too perfect to pass up.

I soon started work as a sales rep, dressed up as a rainbow, accompanied by Kermit the Frog, singing "Rainbow Connection" (which incidentally is  still one of my favorite songs). My unorthodox approach proved surprisingly successful and I went on to create my own sales organization. I named the group Parrot Productions so we could dress in casual and colorful clothes instead of business suits (I needed an alibi at the time). Our calling cards were Plastic Eggs with fun messages inside. I traveled with balloons, gave out giant chocolate chip cookies and showed up with bagels and cream cheese for early morning appointments. I was famous for delightful customer service and fun; and because of it, inspired friendship and loyalty in people.

My customers felt acknowledged and responded by giving me as much of their business as they could (there's a limit to how many striped name patches one needs). The best thing about approaching sales this way is that it made it fun for me and my customers. I very rarely dreaded a sales call because of the relationships that I had established. Who throws out a salesperson carrying a bag of hot bagels?

By the time my children were born, I retired from that line of work and moved on to other things. I got more deeply involved with my spiritual interests, ran children's programs and raised my own kids.

Even though it is in my nature to go toward joy whenever I can, it is not always easy. In fact there was a period when I felt so cut off from my playful self, I believed I would never contact it again. It was a very dark time for me. I made a cross country move, dissolved my marriage and left my spiritual community, all which shook the foundations of everything I believed in at the time. It turned out to be a period of deep introspection. I learned to use the turmoil and suffering to evaluate whether the conventional, ordinary life I had been brought up to believe in was really going to make me happy. I realized the source of my needs for nurturing, belonging and acceptance were legitimate, but the way I had been taught to fulfill them had never touched me in a deep way. To reach real depth in myself, I knew I needed to examine my own soul and have the faith to travel my own path.

I started to choose joy from a very deep place, as a way to be in life and relationship. I began looking at my children and work with an eye for how we could learn happily, in celebration and delight. How could work be approached differently and how could we create celebrations and rituals that help us all grow? I began to practice what I now know to be my mission in life. I finally did create a fabulous Fairy Godmother costume, and on occasion took to the streets asking people about their fondest wishes and visions for their lives. I noticed that most people hadn't given much thought to what they wanted (or maybe they didn't anticipate fairy dust with their muffler estimate). If we don't give our dreams a thought form, how will they ever manifest in life? Over the course of the next number of years I created celebration rituals, gifts, and delightful occasions, both in my personal life and for individual clients.

I came to live my point of view, not because it's been easy for me, but because it's true. It's been a tremendous struggle to have the courage to live my vision fully and not just be myself as a sideline hobby. For me, there have always been two selves standing side by side. There is the playful unorthodox self who goes her own way, and the self that longs to fit in, yearning for acceptance and approval. There is the Fairy Godmother sprinkling fairy dust and asking about wishes and dreams; next to her is Cinderella in the basement, wearing metatarsal arch supports. There is the voice of creativity and courage that is loud and strong, and the voice of resignation and disappointment that moans with frustration. The path to freedom, joy and authenticity is never a clear one, and is often strewn with clumsy obstacles. Either we keep tripping over them or we learn to fly. I prefer to fly!

I believe the quest to become fully ourselves is the most challenging one there is. My lesson has been to learn deep respect and gratitude for what I have to give. You cannot reinvent yourself to fit into all of life's situations - nor should you try. We all have unique talents that will manifest in different ways throughout our lives. It is a disservice to the Divine and to yourself to ignore or turn your back on the gifts you have been blessed with. Each of us has a necessary and valuable contribution to make, and we all have something to teach and learn from each other. If you don't offer your unique piece, who then will do it for you?

This book represents my heartfelt desire to share what I have learned about approaching things a little differently. It is about igniting that spark of originality in you, and helping you to discover new ways to express your creativity and love with delight, surprise and humor, for these are your own personal doorways to joy.

I know we all have deep challenges we wake to each day. I am in no way diminishing or making light of that. Rather, I am suggesting that we also wake up to our own brilliance, our imagination, the breath in our bodies, our strength, the love in our hearts, and the opportunity to make our lives magnificent. Our time here with each other is brief. Let's use it to deepen our love and open to new possibilities.

This book is all about bringing out a sense of appreciation, gratitude, kindness and humor regardless of where you find yourself in your life circumstances at this moment. It is filled with hundreds of ideas, celebrations, inspirations and gifts that can be accomplished easily and beautifully for very little, if any, expense. My intention is to give everyone the experience of abundance, and feeling capable of doing great things. Start anywhere you wish and just keep on sailing through. It is an offering of love from me to each one of you.

These days you will find me dressed up as an angel (I have learned to fly!) encouraging and accompanying you along the way. Something along the lines of Glenda the Good Witch Gone Mad. She is my own personal rendition of my Fairy Godmother dream.

So Bippity Boppity Boo, I've come to play with you!

Section Two

Creating Beautiful Gifts

*that will melt your heart...
Tin Man, are you listening?*

Why Give Gifts?

Gifting is a beautiful art.
Everyone loves to be the recipient, as well as the giver of wonderful gifts. There is some way in which we long to express ourselves, give something of ourselves, and let someone know how we feel about them. There have been times when I have been so overwhelmed with love and appreciation for someone, I have been jumping out of my skin looking for a way to express it.

I am famous for gift giving, or should I say notorious. I can honestly say (and my family and friends can attest to it) that no one has ever received anything from me that was remotely practical, that they ever knew existed, or that was to be found in a store. When I went back home and visited a childhood friend, she took me on a tour of the gifts I had given her over the years. I had forgotten so many of them. She had magic wizards hanging, bottles of potions, and a mad assortment of colorful, fun handmade things. I had made the world and a solar system out of material that hung from the ceiling, and a portable white picket fence for a friend who was missing the security of a conventional life. I have rewritten newspaper headlines making celebrities and heroes out of my friends and filled them with my own inspirational and good news stories. I have planted paper heart seeds that grew into magical trees overnight (snuck in at 5:00 a.m.) as well as making every gift in this chapter.

What all of these gifts have in common though (I know there is a theme in here somewhere) is that they represent a reinforcement or acknowledgment of the recipient and what they were affirming or wishing for in their lives in that moment.

In our travels, I think we are always on the lookout for that perfect gift to give someone. The one that will melt your heart, make you giggle and bring tears to yours eyes—the one that you will hold onto and cherish forever. Well it's not necessarily in the Sunday supplements, because only you know that special ingredient or thought that you want to communicate, or that someone else longs to hear.

In a workshop I was giving, I once asked this question, "What is the best gift you have ever given, and what is the best gift you have ever received?" Everyone had different answers. One man said, "Unconditional love and acceptance is the best gift I've given," and "Unconditional love and acceptance is the best gift I have ever received." When he shared that, everyone looked at their gift list and realized that regardless of what they had chosen as their answer, the elements were the same. In being the recipient, as well as the giver of this treasured gift, they had been seen, loved and appreciated. Whether it was a surprise party, a book, an adventure, or piece of clothing, someone had touched their heart by really noticing and caring about who they were. Interestingly enough, not one person chose a gift that was even slightly monetarily extravagant. Not one!

So what are the gifts in this Chapter about? They are about acknowledging, humoring and loving someone. Sometimes it's hard to express yourself. You feel shy and much too vulnerable.

Depending on your mood and the form of your relationship, there is a gift here, that can help you "find your way in." There is a place where you can safely and freely express yourself. You can make your gifts as intimate, humorous or inspiring as you choose. There are gifts for every occasion and every budget. Keep in mind that nothing of real value has to ever be costly. You can create memorable, cherished treasures for the most significant occasions with a little time and thought. Every one of these gifts has been given time and time again, and the response has always been overwhelmingly positive.

Do you ever miss playing with crayons and paints? Making potions and getting messy? When was the last time you really created a fabulous surprise gift? Do you remember the great presents you would make at school and then wrap and hide with so much glee? Do you steer away from making gifts these days because you feel:

❏ I don't have the time.	❏ A lot of these gifts can be created in one hour or less.
	❏ Figure out shopping time, parking, traffic, tolls, and try to beat that!
❏ It requires more talent and imagination than you can muster up.	❏ You have more talent and imagination than you know. You just need a little help with ideas and inspiration.
❏ I don't know where to begin.	❏ I'll show you how to begin, how to create, and how to deliver the finished product.
❏ It feels totally overwhelming.	❏ Being one who can get overwhelmed at three choices of ice cream, never mind 31 flavors, all of the gifts are broken down into easy bite sized chunks.

The first gift is a bag of quotes that was done by a woman I know. She was invited to a friend's 50th birthday party that was to be a really special occasion. At the time, she had to keep her budget in mind, which was slim, but she also wanted to create something for this woman. She came upon the idea of giving her an inspiring thought for every

15

year of her life. She went to the bookstore and library with a pad of paper and a pen and browsed through the books to find the quotes she thought her friend would love. She copied them on small pieces of beautiful paper and rubber-stamped them with hearts and other fun stamps she had around. She folded each one over, sealed it with a star, put all of them in a beautifully decorated angel bag and went to the party.

I was at the party and saw her friend's response to the gift. She was absolutely delighted. (As a matter of fact, we have her quote in the book.)

So have fun, find something delightful that catches your eye and go for it.

Inspirational quotes

THE THEME

Favorite quotes, priceless sayings, inspirational tidbits. These things make you feel good just to hear them. Package and share them as a beautiful gift that will long be remembered. This is a wonderful idea for a benchmark birthday, a special anniversary, or for someone who is going through a trying time and could use a lift. A lovely gift for all occasions requiring some time, nice stationary and cards, and almost no expense.

> *For my 50th birthday, I received a beautiful bag decorated with angels. Inside the bag were inspirational quotes on little pieces of rubber-stamped cards. There was one for every year of my life. I put it on my dresser and looked forward to reading one thought every day. It touched my heart in a way that no store-bought gift ever could.*
>
>   ✍ *CONNIE P.*

MATERIALS

Research of Quotes:

First you'll need to collect a large assortment of quotes. This is actually quite easily done. There are books of quotes available at the library, as well as bookstores. I have actually gone into both (shhh!) and with a notebook copied down my favorite quotes. When you have enough of them, you can begin putting your gift together.

Cards to Use:

Any type of small card will do. You can cut paper out or go to an office supply house and buy sheets of small cards, business card size. You can also go to a copy place and buy card stock that you can cut up, or find some lovely stationary with envelopes that you might like to use. Blank florist cards work well and have their own envelopes.

Decorations and Closure for the Cards:

Rubber stamps, stickers and/or colored markers are all you need for this project. You can decorate the cards any way you choose. Close the quotes by folding them over and using scotch tape, tiny hearts, or gold stars, available at any office supply store. If the cards come with envelopes, you can just seal them and decorate the envelope.

Writing Instrument:

Any nice pen or marker works well. Colored markers or a gold pen look especially beautiful.

CREATING THE GIFT

☙ *Write out all of the quotes on your chosen stationary, and decorate them in any way you like. When you have completed them, you will need something to put the quotes in. Beautiful party bags or boxes work well. I have even used Chinese take-out containers available at party stores in different colors and designs.*

☙ *Decorate the outside of the bag or container with something that says Inspirational Quotes or put a sticker or label on it and write Inspirational Quotes on that. I wrap the box in cellophane, tie it up with a ribbon and attach a trinket, candy stick or something fun on the outside.*

SHOPPING

Use office supply stores for cards, pens and markers. In party stores you'll find boxes, bags, stickers and cellophane.

CREATIVE OPTIONS

If you choose to make a number of these gifts for friends, you can write your quotes on the computer and copy them. Cut them out and use them for all of your boxes or bags.

If you would like to elaborate or play with this, you can choose quotes by categories or themes — Valentine's Day — Put together love quotes or love poetry. Package them in a heart-shaped bag or box with hearts, or any pretty Valentine's package. You can wrap the whole thing in cellophane with hearts and attach a beautiful chocolate or trinket on top.

- *Get Well Gift — Find quotes of hope and inspiration. Put them in cheerful packaging with a note to open them on a daily (or even more frequent) basis.*

- *Thank You Gifts, Christmas, Anniversaries, Birthdays, Friendship, or an Anytime Gift — Find quotes on appreciation, gratitude, friendship and love and package them attractively.*

- *Baby Gift — Select quotes on children, patience, love, growth and challenge. Wrap them up in a beautiful baby bag with a little toy attached to the top.*

- *Jobs, Promotions, or how about a Job Seeker? Use quotes on striving, faith and excellence. There are so many people discouraged out there that could really use it. Help them take the next great leap in their lives.*

🕊 *Death of a Loved One* — *Often times after the initial period of bereavement, a person is left pretty much to themselves to grieve. It can be quite a lonely time. Though you cannot be there on a daily basis, words of encouragement can be. Put together a selection of encouraging, deeply heart felt quotes for a friend to open whenever they could use a lift.*

PREPARATION

Outside of collecting the quotes, the gift requires just the time it takes to write them out and package them. A nice gift should take you about an hour for each one depending upon the content of the quotes and the amount of quotes you use.

Prescriptions for life

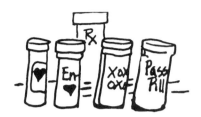

THE THEME

Don't you wish you had the antidote for what *ails* you in life? How about the elixir for the 4 P's: Power, Patience, Permission, Pleasure?

Turn yourself into your own neighborhood pharmacist and start filling those prescriptions with an incredible variety of ideas and remedies for parents, lovers, friends and kids. Everything you need is here to create and dispense (minus the board license). Join the Prescription of the Month Club. Fun for everyone and a compassionate loving response to some difficult areas in one's life.

> *I received this gift one year for Christmas packaged as a small medicine chest. I have always had a particularly hard time giving myself permission to express anger, and also giving myself permission to let more pleasure and fun in my life. This gift contained all of these little medicine bottles. I got power pills, anger pills, pleasure pills and a few others. The 'pleasure pill bottle' said that there was 'a lifetime prescription that I could refill endlessly.' 'Pills guaranteed to expand and never contract.'*
>
> *You know, it's funny, I lay them on my dresser and I pop a few now and then. It's been a great reminder to me. It took issues that were difficult for me and made them less serious. I really loved this present.*
>
> ✍ BRIAN D.

21

MATERIALS

- ☐ *Empty vial jars, available at most pharmacies*
- ☐ *Labels to stick on*
- ☐ *Jelly beans, gum drops, mints or favorite candy to fill up bottles*

SHOPPING

A pharmacy could do it all, although you might like to go to a candy store for a better *pill* selection.

CREATING THE GIFT

Fill the bottles with assorted candies and decide what the labels will say. Choose a name for your pharmacy such as Dr. Spock, Dr. Strangelove, or Dr. Seuss, or choose some other funny name as the prescribing physician. Decide what type of  prescription it is and write out the instructions you like, such as, Never runs out, Guaranteed to work immediately, Take with 2 hugs and 2 kisses, or F.O.D. (filled on demand).

Once you have written the labels, put them directly onto the bottles. Here are some ideas for prescriptions:

1. *PERMISSION PILLS* – *giving you permission to do what is hard, whether it is to have more fun, let go of something difficult or embrace something new*

2. *POWER AND STRENGTH PILLS* – *for those times when you're just feeling a little too weak to cope*

3. *PLEASURE PILLS* – *to allow extra pleasure in your life that you ordinarily wouldn't; to embrace joy*

22

4. *RELAXATION PILLS* – take 2 anytime you feel yourself getting stressed out and crazy. Works instantaneously.

5. *AFFECTION PILLS* – for those times when it's hard to reach out

6. *GIGGLING GUM DROPS OR HUMOR PILLS* – Laugh more in life. Overdosing is impossible.

7. *PMS PILLS* – you write the script!!

8. *DELIGHT PILLS* – for added enjoyment and pleasure

MORE CREATIONS

Okay, go for broke. You can create a whole pharmacy with this. Get a cardboard box and create a humorous medicine cabinet. Fill it up with all sorts of remedies. Get really playful with it.

For Parents:
⊙ *PATIENCE PILLS*—guaranteed to never run out

For Dancers or Wanna Be Dancers:
⊙ *RIGHT FOOT PILLS*—for someone with two left feet

For Lovers:
⊙ *FANTASY PRESCRIPTION* —x-rated, how about something really funny and sexy
⊙ *POTENCY PILLS*—for long lasting relief
⊙ *LACK OF INHIBITION*—for daring feats not previously attempted

Co-Workers:
⊙ *BIG PILLS* — for when you are feeling petty and small
⊙ *GOSSIP REMEDIES* — guaranteed to nip it in the bud
⊙ *PASS THE BUCK REMEDIES* — don't even take the time to swallow

Sales People:

⊙ *QUOTA PILLS—guaranteed to keep you running. Prescription: It is never enough.*

Dating:

⊙ *TONGUE-TIED PILLS—guaranteed to relieve first night stammering and jitters*

Politicians and Others:

⊙ *CONSCIENCE PILLS—when you forget you have one*
⊙ *CONSOLATION PILLS*

CREATIVE OPTIONS

You could create a Prescription of the Month Club for whatever comes up in your relationship and create the antidote for it.

APPROPRIATE FOR
All occasions.

PREPARATION

Just a few minutes needed to fill the bottles and label them if you have the idea. A nice pharmacy should take around an hour.

Matisse, if you please, pass the paints...

body paints

THE THEME

This is a gift of body paints made out of sauces, spreads and chocolate. Body painting is a wonderful way to loosen up and have fun. This is a fun, erotic and playful gift that would delight any lover. Usually you only see these types of spreads or paints at sex stores or lingerie shops, or party stores. They go under various names like love potions, or chocolate body paints. They are usually quite expensive and are so simple to create. Hey, why should Frederick's make all the profit and get all the glory?

> *Do you remember the old 'Laugh In' show where Goldie Hawn was dressed in a bathing suit and she was at a dance party? Her whole body was covered with these wild designs and they would zoom in on her and she would giggle. That body painting fascinated me. I once found these great paint crayons that you could draw all over your body with, and then they would easily wash off, but I haven't seen them around for years. So here is an alternative to have some fun with. You can probably still hear the echo from your mother's voice 'Don't play with your food!' Well mom, move over, the time has come. Here is a recipe for a great gift to play with.*

MATERIALS

Spreads to Use:

♥ *You can buy spreads already available (yes!). These can be anything from: Chocolate fudge sauces (Hershey's never looked so enticing*

♥ *Ice cream toppings*

♥ *Sugarless jams and jellies*

♥ *Fruit-sweetened chocolate*

♥ *There are also many low-fat or fat-free versions on the market (as if this would make a difference)!*

Containers and Labels:

★ *Sticky labels or beautiful stickers with room to write on*

★ *Empty bottles you've collected (if you are making your own spreads or want to transfer a spread to a different bottle.) Beautiful bottles are also available at houseware stores.*

★ *A small dime store paintbrush*

★ *Cellophane and ribbon for wrapping*

★ *A nice writing instrument, or if you have a computer, you can create your labels on the computer*

CREATING THE GIFT

Have a clean bottle in front of you. If you are using store bought spreads, soak the bottles to remove the original labels from the jars and then you are all set to go. Have the unlabeled jars in front of you. Create your own messages to put on the labels.

The Ultimate Body Paint

Examples:
- ♥ *John's Private Reserve Body Paint,
  Vintage 1995*
- ♥ *The Ultimate Body Paint For
  My Ultimate Man/Woman*
- ♥ *Diane's Chocolate Body Paint
  (to be used only on one canvas – Mine!),
  Expiration Date: _____*

When you are done writing out the label, attach your label to the jar. You can also add little stickers to the jar if you want it to look fancier. Take cellophane and wrap it up, tying it with a ribbon, and attach one or two dime store paintbrushes on the top. You can enclose a tag with an invitation to use it on a specific date.

CREATIVE OPTIONS
If you are a cook or would like to create your own recipes for spreads, go wild. Make red and green spreads for Christmas or special Valentine's Day spreads, or give one at a birthday with a new vintage date on it.

APPROPRIATE FOR...
This is a gift for lovers. It is appropriate for birthdays, anniversaries, Valentine's Day, I love you, and no doggone apparent reason.

PREPARATION
15 minutes for store bought spreads, 1 hour or longer for homemade.

If I could keep time in a bottle...

THE THEME

This gift is a representation of your desire and commitment to spend more time with the significant people in your life and to focus on your priorities. Learn how to create More Time Together, or Time to Listen for your lover or child. Are you worn out with a life full of responsibility? Make yourself a bottle of Time and Energy.

We'll show you how to hold back the sands of time and in the process create a memorable gift for you and your loved ones. That's the last time you will hear, "I'm late, I'm late, no time to say hello, goodbye, I'm late, I'm late, I'm late." You'll never run short of time again. This is a bottle filled with the sands of time easily created, inexpensive and applicable for all relationships.

> *I have a theory about time. I think that there is a time thief that stalks lovers and other joy- producing activities. When you don't watch for it, it sneaks up behind you. For instance, my time thief always shows up on my most pleasurable days, but never shows up at a baseball game. I could sit in a stadium for the rest of my life and never grow old. I'm convinced the day would never pass. Just like when I was in elementary school and I swear the hands on the clock never moved between 3:20 and 3:30 which was our dismissal time. For you of course, baseball might be a great joy and that time thief is sitting beside you on the bleachers munching a hot dog as we speak, and stealing homebase. So here is your opportunity to play with time, to expand it and make it a great friend, and to delight someone with your intention to be more available.*

29

MATERIALS

- Any kind of beautiful glass bottle, preferably with a cork (available at kitchen stores, some hardware stores and gift stores)

- Sand from outside or colored sand available at pet stores or craft stores

- A small card to attach to the bottle

- Labels for the jar or stickers with a nice design that fits the bottle with instructions

- A tag for instructions

- Cellophane or any other type of wrapping paper (clear paper looks best)

CREATING THE GIFT

- Take the bottles and fill them with sand from the beach, a sand box, or use some colored sand if you like from the pet or hobby store. In a pinch, you can use rice kernels, corn meal or flour.

- Decide what you want on the label. Some ideas would be:
  - ★ *Extra Time for Everything you Want*
  - ★ *No More Wasted Time*
  - ★ *More Time Together*
  - ★ *Time for What's Important*
  - ★ *Time for All of the Important Things*
  - ★ *Time and Energy*
  - ★ *Precious Time with You*
  - ★ *Time to Listen*

🕊 Label the bottles and take a tag and write out some instructions on it. It could say:

★ *Here is more time together with the person I Love, guaranteed to never run out;*

★ *Time for you to do all of the wonderful things you love, completely unavailable to the time thief;*

★ *Precious time – anyone who tries to steal it will be prosecuted to the full extent of the law, signed, (father/mother/brother/sister/time).*

MORE CREATIONS

💜 Lovers: Precious Time with You, Time for Intimacy, and Endless Time Together

💜 Friends: More Time Together or More Time to Share

💜 Parent: Time to Yourself or Time to Relax

💜 Child: Time to Listen, Time to Play, Time for Fun

APPROPRIATE FOR
Anyone.

PREPARATION
15 minutes or so.

A Treasure Box of Memories

THE THEME

Have you ever given any thought to what it is you really love and treasure about the people close to you? Maybe it's time for you to think about it. What delightful excursions, talks, moments and memories unite you? Can you imagine putting them all together and presenting them as a gift? It's an unbelievable treasure! Completed, it is a testament of your love and the value you place on your relationship. This is one of the most remarkable gifts you can give anyone, especially for significant occasions, anniversaries, birthdays and holidays.

My friend was planning a birthday celebration for her husband. We cooked up a wonderful creation of an Italian bistro on the patio outside. We talked about gifts and I suggested she put an appreciation box together for her husband. They have been together quite awhile and have lots of significant memories and feelings to share. She commented on the fact that her husband was the more likely of the two of them to express his feelings and to share them on paper. She said she was not as sentimentally inclined. She wrote down memories of wonderful occasions and trips they had had together as well as her thoughts of all of the things she loved and appreciated about him. She then color-coded them for past memories and special thoughts. On the day of the celebration, she wrapped up her treasure chest and offered it to him as a gift. She said she had rarely seen him as moved, and the impact was immense. When she found the box a few days later, she opened it and saw that it was totally empty. He had taken every piece of paper and put them away.

I have given this gift to three significant people in my life. I gave it at Christmas time to my partner. I wrote about 50 different ways in which I loved him, the things I noticed about him and what I treasured about him. With tears in his eyes, he told me it was one of the most important gifts he had ever received.

The other 2 treasure boxes I made for my children. I kept a little notebook and wrote down things about each of them I saw and appreciated. At Christmas, I put them all on beautiful paper in small envelopes and decorated a beautiful box. My 11-year old looked at me when she was reading them and said, 'I never realized you noticed that and paid so much attention to me.' My teenage daughter loved it and created one for her dad's birthday.

We often say that our lives are made up by our memories and by sharing them. They become richer and more alive when we demonstrate the gratitude that we have in relationships with each other. The questions to ask yourself as you put this gift together would be:

1. *What do you love about the recipient of this gift?*

2. *What delightful things, excursions, talks and moments have you shared?*

3. *What are some of the best times you have had together?*

4. *The most poignant?*

5. *The most meaningful?*

MATERIALS

★ *Your thoughts, fondest memories and feelings*

★ *A beautiful box, treasure chest box or any type of a bag to put the cards in (available at a party store). Large cardboard pirate treasure chests are usually available at party stores and work well.*

★ *Small cards with envelopes or pieces of paper to write on*

★ *Rubber stamps or stickers to decorate the gift, and stickers for closures if you don't have envelopes*

CREATING THE GIFT

✍ *This is a gift that requires time and thought. What you are doing is creating an appreciation log of the relationship you share together. Look through scrapbooks, photo albums, cards, etc. to jar your memory. You can even write your memories by the years in which they occurred. Start remembering the things that you share together and begin to write them out on paper.*

✍ *Be generous. Write down special moments you have had, times that have meant a lot, something funny you recall, or a time when you felt particularly loved.*

✍ *For an old friend it could be something like: Remember when we were in high school and we spent all day playing together in the snow and we came home soaking wet and drank three cups of hot chocolate. Or it could be: Remember when we both found out that we were accepted to the same college and talked for two hours about our plans and what to pack.*

❧ *For Parents – Remember the night our daughter was born and we sat in the silence of the night rocking her and holding hands? The world never felt as safe or beautiful. I remember feeling so close to you.*

❧ *Write each one out on a piece of paper and put it in the box. You can even color-code them. For instance, trips you have taken can be one color; memories you have with each other can be another color; things around children can be another color; or love and appreciation can be done in another color.*

❧ *Fill the box with the cards you have written. When your box is filled, label it and wrap it beautifully. It will become a most cherished gift.*

MORE CREATIONS

This is a gift that is lovely for many relationships. If you are creating a few of these at a time, let's say for a holiday or family gift, here is my suggestion.

1. *Get a sorting tool to use:*
   A file folder
   A small recipe box
   Even a shoe bag with
   12 different pockets

2. *Use different colored papers for each person, in case you get mixed up. Start looking through photo albums. Pull out the photographs that you wish to share and get a copy made. Photo albums help to stir memories. Whenever you have a fond memory, write it down in a small notebook if you are not home. Or if you are home, write it out immediately and slip it into the pocket or place you've designated. Then, putting them together is a simple affair.*

APPROPRIATE FOR...

- ♥ *Partners, Lovers and Spouses:*
    Anniversary gifts
    Valentine's Day
    Birthdays
    Because I Love You
- ♥ *Parents/Siblings:*
    For Family Reunions
    Special Anniversaries
    Significant Holidays
    Family Projects
- ♥ *Children:*
    Graduation gifts
    Coming of age
    Significant transitions
    Leaving home
    Marriage
- ♥ *Co-Workers:*
    Celebrating a promotion
    Leaving a job
    Retiring
    Moving away
- ♥ *Neighbors or Friends:*
    Moving away
    Anniversaries
    Holiday celebrations

Special Note:
- ♥ *The Death of a Loved One:*
    This is a great gift to a family when a loved one dies. Gather friends and relatives together to contribute a few special memories of that person and give it to the family after the initial deep period of bereavement is over.

PREPARATION

Time involved varies too much to say. Once you have your memories on paper, it should take less than ½ hour to fill your treasure chest, label and wrap it.

I wish I may, I wish I might ...

wishing pouches

THE THEME

The main theme here is a beautiful pouch that can be worn, hung on your wall or carried in your pocket that holds your deepest wishes, dreams, affirmations, prayers and hopes in written or symbolic form. This is a significant *YES* statement to the universe and a gift that supports every vision someone has in their lives for themselves and others. A great gift for all occasions and you don't need to be a Home Ec graduate. If you can sew a straight line, you are all set (it wouldn't kill the looks of it for it to be crooked either).

This is a gift I have given many friends. All of us have wishes and dreams. This is a wonderful way to celebrate and affirm each of our desires in life.

> *On a date close to Christmas, my friend told me about a gift she had received from a woman she had just met. It was a small pendant which was engraved with the words, Protect this Woman. When I heard this, I thought it was the most wonderful thing to receive, it being a time in my life when I was feeling particularly vulnerable. I wished I had been with her, when she met this woman so that I might have been given one too. I longed to have such a special symbol of protection.*

> *On Christmas day, my friend gifted me with the most beautiful red wishing pouch containing wishes for my health and happiness and attached to the outside of the pouch was the pendant, Protect this Woman. I was moved very deeply by this. Without me ever telling her, she knew how much I wanted and needed it. It was a gift from the heart filled with love, caring and nurturing. I felt truly loved and blessed.*

> ✍ ANNE S.

39

We used our wishing pouch at our wedding to put our rings in.

✍ GWEN G.

I keep my wishing pouch by my bed and sometimes put it under my pillow when there is something I'm strongly working toward.

✍ JOHN C.

On New Year's, I put all my dreams, affirmations and goals for the coming year along with my own blessings and prayers for others in it.

✍ SUSAN R.

MATERIALS

* *A piece of velvet fabric or any beautiful material you wish to use*
* *A silver or gold fabric pen*
* *Glue glitter or any other decorative glitter (optional)*
* *A tasseled rope*
* *An amulet, special bead or charm for the closure*
* *Thread to match the material*
* *A sewing machine or you can sew it by hand*

CREATING THE GIFT

To make the pouch, cut out your own pattern or trace the one below and enlarge it. The pouch can be of any size, but if you make it small, you can wear it, put it in your pocket or hang it on the wall. It helps if you know how to sew a little. A beginner can easily tackle this project though; if you can sew a button or a straight line, you're in.

Sewing instructions:

Figure 1: Cut out 2 pieces of fabric the same size and attach right sides together using the above pattern. Sew across bottom edge and top flap. Sew up sides to notch. Leave enough space open to turn pouch inside out (so you can see the velvet). Sew closed the space you left open.

Figure 2: Fold bottom up to flap to make a pouch. Sew up sides.

Figure. 3: Turn inside out again and velvet pouch will be completed with the flap.

Figure 4: Sew on amulet. Sew on braided cord. Decorate with fabric markers.

For my closures, I use anything that reminds me of that person or what they love. You can pick up great charms at a bead store. You can use the person's astrological sign, a heart, something of sentimental value, a bead from a piece of clothing or perhaps an animal that they like.

In gold fabric pen, I write down their name and say, So and so's wishes and dreams. You can also add a piece of paper inside with an inscription of how you feel or what you hope for them.

Examples:

> *This is a place to put all of your wishes and dreams and to keep them close to your heart. I hope all of your dreams come true.*

> *May all your wishes and dreams come alive. I cheer you on and wish only for your highest happiness.*

Come up with something that feels and sounds right to you.

CREATIVE OPTIONS

You can create a different theme for things that you want. They are great for work dreams or wishes for intimacy. For instance, if you have a friend who would love an intimate relationship, they could place inside the pouch what they value and hope for and affirm for themselves in that relationship.

APPROPRIATE FOR...

Lovers/partners:
Affirmations for your relationship. Things you want to create in life together.

Children:
Great affirmations for kids to know you reinforce them. A positive yes statement in life. Help them focus on what they want in life and what is possible!

Friends:
All occasions, birthdays are wonderful.

Marriage or Engagement Gifts:
A wonderful wedding gift for each partner.

For our wedding, we received a basket with gifts that included a wishing pouch for each of us to put our dreams in. It really got us thinking and feeling what we wanted to create, both for ourselves and each other.

✍ JUDY R.

Birth of Children:
What a wonderful way to welcome a baby. You can give the gift with your wishes of well-being for the child and then pass it on to be filled by the parents to add their own wishes for that child.

PREPARATION

An hour or so with a sewing machine. Add an extra 30 - 45 minutes for hand sewing.

Certificates of Appreciation

THE THEME

Have you ever been acknowledged for a quality, achievement, or a talent you have that you are really proud of? Not something that merely recognized your competitive edge, but something that appreciated your true gifts. This is a certificate that appreciates the unique qualities of the recipient, that can be handmade and framed or laminated as a treasured keepsake. A great gift for teachers, parents, friends, co-workers or partners.

When I was working for a sales organization, I had a manager with a delightful sense of fun and appreciation. The company used to have all of these little sales contests and have occasions when they would give out plaques. There was one time at the end of the project where I was awarded two plaques for sales excellence which, to be truthful, in that particular circumstance didn't mean that much to me.

At the same time, my manager made awards of excellence for everyone that had to do with what she really saw about us. They were humorous, poignant and truthful. Which plaque do you think I put up on my wall? What do you think I really wanted to be reminded of? One was competition based—I win and you lose. The other was all of the unique qualities that she saw in all of us. When I left my job, that was the last thing to leave my wall. Some people are naturally good at inspiration. Incidentally, her group always outperformed others and with much more fun thrown in. She inspired such tremendous loyalty that I, for one, was relieved when she quit because I felt permission to finally leave too.

How many of us have certificates hanging up on the wall? Degrees? Diplomas? What would you really like to be valued and appreciated for? This is a delightful gift that can be given to anyone at any time. One year this was our Christmas gift to my children's teachers and you can't imagine how delighted they were with it. My daughter went back to visit one of her teachers, and it was still hanging on his bulletin board three years later.

Stop and think of someone you love. What are the qualities that you appreciate about them? For instance,

- *You're always taking time to listen to me*
- *Your kindnesses*
- *The way you always hug me*
- *The courage you show everyday*
- *Your careful attention when you drive*
- *The delicious meals you prepare for me*
- *The way you work so hard to support us*

MATERIALS

- ★ *Large, thick paper*
- ★ *Markers or colored pens*
- ★ *A computer (optional)*
- ★ *Laminating the certificate (optional)*
- ★ *A frame (optional)*

CREATING THE GIFT

On a scrap piece of paper, list ten or so qualities (or more, if they can fit) you appreciate and love about this person. Make up the heading for the certificate. You can call it: Certificate of Appreciation or I Honor and Acknowledge You For _____, or You Are Unbelievably Special to Me Because of the Following Reasons .... And make sure you leave a place for their name at the top.

Then list them any way that you like on the certificate. You can decorate it, using colored markers, or have it look more formal if you create it on a computer. Once this is done, you can have it laminated at the copy store, or frame it. This gift will be held onto and cherished forever.

APPROPRIATE FOR…

Lovers/Partners:

Your loving nature, Your incredible desire and passion, The way you always compliment me, Rooting for me in life.

Teachers:

Your great enthusiasm, The way you always help and encourage me, The way you make history so interesting, The way you listen to me.

Kids:

The great effort you put out in sports, The great way you take care of your pets, Your loving energy towards your siblings, The way you always hug me.

Friends:

Your listening ear, Sharing my deepest dreams and sorrows, Bringing over pizza and laughing with me when the world seems grim.

Co-Workers/Anyone Else You Deal With in the Public:

Excellent service, Your attention to detail, Taking good care of my car (hence, me).

PREPARATION TIME

An hour or so depending on decorations.

The Quote of the Week

THE THEME

This gift combines our love of fun tidbits, wisdom and inspirational sayings with the delight of receiving personal handwritten mail. Find a wealth of meaningful quotes and personalize the gift for those going through a difficult passage, loss, illness, or a discouraging time, or maybe just as a way to stay in touch with loved ones.

This is an ongoing gift of inspiration on the lines of the Book of the Month Club or when I was a kid, my dad's favorite gift, the Cheese of the Month Club. (Incidentally, don't mail gorgonzola cheese ever.) Something that uplifts the spirit that you can look forward to all year long.

Make someone the recipient of your thoughts or inspirational quotes and send them every week.

MATERIALS

- ♥ *A collection of inspirational quotes you like*
- ♥ *Postcards or cards*
- ♥ *Postage*

CREATING THE GIFT

Send a gift card and let someone know that your gift to them is a quote for the week that they will be receiving all year round. Gather some plain cards or postcards so that you have them ready to send. Every time you hear or see a great inspirational thought, write it down on one of the cards. Choose one day of the week that you always mail it out on and every week mail that person an inspirational thought. Keep it up as a year-long gift, a summer gift or for months at a time. I actually did this with a group of friends of mine where I sent out 2 or 3 cards a week for a number of months.

Quotes are available from all sources. There are even books of quotes that you can buy. Or just browse through your own books, or go to the library.

There are so many times during the day that you always hear something special—a joke, or something that somebody says that really touches you. Keep a small notebook around so you can easily write them down and have them on hand.

APPROPRIATE FOR...

Lovers/Partners:

Even if you live together, this is a great gift to send in the mail. Wouldn't you love to receive an inspiring thought in your mailbox. You can keep it posted until the following one arrives.

Friends:

To let them know you are thinking of them, to inspire each other as you go for your dreams.

Faraway Loved Ones:

A great way to keep your friendship alive, positive and encouraging.

Friends Going Through Loss, Illness or Bereavement:

Inspirational quotes to help them move through transition and keep a positive vision in front of them.

Kids:

Quotes from people they admire or people who have accomplished a lot even under great adversity. Help keep children positive and motivated even in the difficult times, especially when it is hard for them to listen to you.

PREPARATION

A few minutes each week to write out the quote and mail it.

Raindrops keep falling on my head...

showers of delight

THE THEME

Bath, shampoo and body products are yummy. They smell delicious, are a visual treat, and they make you feel taken care of and pampered. Wouldn't you love to shower in delight, or create a shower of warmth and appreciation? Wouldn't it be fun to show up at baby and wedding showers, and steal everyone's heart with your clever imaginative style? Make your own packaged set, personalized for every occasion, taste and style.

I'll show you how to end up smelling like roses at any gathering merely for the price of a bouquet of daisies.

> One of my favorite scenes in a movie is Gene Kelly in 'Singing in the Rain.' I love his joy and the absolute fun of dancing in the rain splashing in puddles while being 'showered on.' Being showered on always creates wonderful images for me – from the rice throwing at wedding celebrations to the blur of confetti, to the more traditional baby and wedding celebrations, where you are basically showered in an abundance of good wishes and gifts.

My kids and I like to listen to James Taylor. One of our favorite songs is 'Shower the People You Love with Love.' One day, I took a spray bottle and filled it with rosewater and hid it while I went to turn on the song. Every time he sang 'shower the people you love with love,' I held the bottle over their heads and showered them with the rosewater. They giggled in delight. (So do my adult friends when I surprise them in the same way.)

The idea of taking something as simple as everyday products and adding the twist of turning them into a blessing and shower, works magnificently.

MATERIALS

- *Tall plastic squeeze bottles (if they are to be kept in the shower or bathroom), available in health food, craft or houseware stores or...*

- *Beautiful glass bottles with corks or screw tops (if they will be kept in a safer, crash-free place), available in craft stores, kitchen stores and some gift stores*

- *Favorite bubble baths, shampoos or bath gels. You can buy them in bulk in health food stores and body shops*

- *Labels or decorative stickers to attach to the bottles*

- *Ribbon*

- *Cellophane for wrapping or any clear wrapping paper (optional but it completes the look)*

- *A little trinket to tie to the gift, e.g. nail brush or comb (optional but looks nice)*

CREATING THE GIFT

You are creating showers of delight! First fill up the bottles with bubble bath, shampoos and bath gels. Take out your labels and think about how you want to label them. Some suggestions—*Showering in Delight, A Shower of Joy for You, You Shower Me with Delight, A Shower of Warmth and Appreciation for You.*

When you have decided what you want it to say, write it out on the label. Then in small print somewhere, write out what the product is (if it is a shampoo or bubble bath or bath gel).

You can also make gift sets as well. Create a whole set of shampoo, bubble bath and bath gel. Add little instructions that might say, You shower me in delight, I would like to shower you in delight, or whatever you think someone would enjoy.

MORE CREATIONS

Baby Gifts:
This is a wonderful gift to shower your baby in delight with. Fill the bottles, in this case with mild, soothing, safe baby products. When you are done, wrap the bottles up in cellophane and attach them with a ribbon on top. They will look beautiful.

APPROPRIATE FOR...
Lovers, friends, and (Surprise, Surprise)--shower gifts for engagements, weddings and baby gifts.

PREPARATION
Half an hour or less for a set.

Spreading Delight

THE THEME

Remember Johnny Appleseed who spent a good part of his life spreading seeds all over the world? Be your own Johnny Appleseed by spreading something wonderful and fun. Find out how to make and spread goodwill, happiness or joy.

Here are some edible versions of all of these spreads combined with delightful ideas that will send you on your journey of goodwill. From the bawdy to the bashful, your toast and jam will never look the same! Suggestions for lovers, friends (and even mothers-in-law).

MATERIALS

- *Store-bought jams, jellies, honey or anything of the sticky, spready variety; or a great homemade recipe for jams or a spread that you are noted for.*

- *Wide-mouthed jars. If the store-bought spreads don't come in an easy wide mouth jar, purchase some in a kitchen store or craft store. Wash them well in hot water.*

- *Beautiful labels, stickers to write on or labels you can decorate.*

- *Cellophane and ribbons for wrapping.*

CREATING THE GIFT

Transfer the spreads to clean, wide-mouthed jars and seal them. Bring out the labels you have chosen. The fun here is in creating the labeling. How about *Spreading Delight All Over You*, *Spreading Happiness*, *Spreading Goodwill*, *Spreading Joy*, or *Spreading My Happiness*. You can put a vintage year on it such as, *Spreading Joy*, *Vintage 1996*, and then wrap up the whole gift in cellophane with a ribbon topping it off.

APPROPRIATE FOR...
Anyone.

PREPARATION
Half an hour or less.

L'eau De Joy...
sprays and potions

THE THEME

Here is the answer we have all been waiting for —
a spray bottle of potions to instantaneously remove
what you don't like or add to what you would like
more of in your life. Learn the secret of spraying
away shame, guilt and fear. All this, presented in a
humorous, loving and accepting fashion, is a gift
that everyone could use and would love to receive.

MATERIALS

★ *Clear spray bottles available at health food
    stores, craft stores, houseware stores and
    probably mail order*

★ *Rosewater or essence of a nice scent
    (lavender)*

★ *Labels*

★ *Tags and strings*

★ *Wrapping paper (cellophane looks great)*

CREATING THE GIFT

OK, what do you want to spray away? Think about
it. Take a bottle and fill it with rosewater or plain
water with a scent added. You can also color the
water very lightly. For instance, Rage be Gone
might be red. The fun part is in labeling it.

Here are a few suggestions:

- *Shame be Gone Spray whenever you feel an attack of shame coming on.*

- *Guilt be Gone To be used for all of those indulgent moments that are so much fun. Keep around for holiday eating, or when you give yourself permission to cross a previously solid boundary.*

- *Remorse be Gone For letting go of the past when it blocks you from present joy.*

- *A Spray of Courage Wouldn't that be a nice perfume line? Liz, are you listening? For those moments we all need a little help.*

- *Write up your own label and put it on the bottle. Then you can add a tag with your own instructions on it such as: To be used when you need a little more courage. Spray as needed. Or for Guilt Be Gone, Spray as soon as you feel an attack coming on. Carry with you at all times.*

- *Punch a hole through the tag and attach with a pretty card. These bottles look great wrapped in cellophane.*

APPROPRIATE FOR...

For anyone when they need more help.

Stress at Jobs, Exam Taking, or Any Challenges:

Fear be Gone, Bewilderment be Gone, A Touch of Humor.

For Kid's Room:

A Breath of Fresh Air? (To be sprayed when the room becomes unbearable)

Far Away Friends:

Miles be Gone (To spray away loneliness)

Friends:

A Splash of Humor,
A Splash of Joy,
A Splash of Courage,
A Splash of Fun.

Politicians and Others:

A Splash of Conscience.

PREPARATION

15 minutes

Section

Three

Follow the Yellow Brick Road... great adventures

Playfulness is part of our intrinsic nature. As children, all of us had more of an opportunity to play. We could go on imaginary expeditions, spend hours in our cardboard forts, radio each other from tin cans in treetops, and spend the whole day on our own private desert islands. We created a world that matched our dreams and when we wanted to go there, we just made it appear. The woods became an enchanted garden, small ponds became oceans to journey across, and a packed picnic became the last bit of food available on a new planet where we landed in our spaceships. Remember the feeling of getting up on a summer or weekend day too busy to eat, bounding out of the house with great plans.

The whole day would pass and it still wasn't long enough for all of the places we longed to go. Where did that childlike enthusiasm disappear? There are still places we all long to visit, languages we would love to learn, and costumes we would love to wear. There are characters to play and heroes we still want to be. If you think this child-like daydreaming goes away when you grow up, look at the surge of activity that surrounds Halloween, one of the fastest growing adult holidays. It is the only culturally sanctioned holiday that gives us permission to assume another identity, and adults are buying unusual and exotic costumes in droves. Who do you usually show up as?

When you wear a costume, you are giving yourself more permission to step out of your usual identity. At the same time, you have the safety of a persona to hide behind. We often show up as a fantasy version of the selves we never quite got the chance to be or the part of ourselves we have hidden because we have never felt it was okay to express it. The NICE girl transforms into the wicked

65

witch, the *SHY, RETIRING* one into the exotic dancer, and the bagger at the grocery store into a shining knight in King Arthur's court. Sometimes we choose a character from a time in history we wish we had lived in. You get to be as outrageous as you please and yet know that no one holds you responsible for your behavior. That brazen, exotic dancer isn't really me, that's Gypsy Rose Lee.

Sometimes we get costumes from a time period in our own past; think of the popularity of 50's parties, of sock hops and classic car parades. Being sixteen again helps us to loosen up and remember our younger, more playful selves. Many of us freeze into a rigid identity of what an adult should be, and then stay frozen like a Popsicle the rest of our lives. What happens to the rest of our potential self?

If you are fortunate and have found a way to be more multifaceted in your day-to-day life, a little more of you gets to be alive on a regular basis. There is the dentist who drills teeth all day, but stars in the local theatre production at night. There is the orthopedic surgeon who spends the month in Jamaica boning up (sorry, couldn't resist) on his steel drumming skills for the jazz combo he performs with. For many of us however, so much is stifled or left undiscovered. The routine of daily life just eats it up. That is why it is so necessary to take the time to discover what else is inside us beside the professional and personal roles we play each day.

Only in our free time can we escape, but it is usually into passive activities where we settle for someone else's escapades and heroics on the screen, like watching television or sitting through a movie, instead of creating our own adventures.

Adventuring is an important part of experience. It is essential to shake up ordinary encounters and put on our dream hats, the ones that take us places we would like to go. If finances permit it (which is rarer than we would like it to be), we might plan a vacation to the Tahitian Islands or someplace else where we have always wanted to go. Usually though, these travel adventures, as wonderful as they are, occur only one week out of the year. The rest of the year, we're at our desk or at the kitchen sink. Why not give yourself the joy and permission to create adventures on an ongoing basis? Why not experience the delight of your own secret hideaway vacations without the responsibilities and expense of leaving home? For me, these adventures began many years ago in college. Since then, over the years, I have participated both personally and professionally in the creation of hundreds of events. Everything from elaborate treasure hunts, to nights in exotic locations. We have had tea or the elaborate Sunday brunch at the Park Plaza in New York. I have taken friends to Paris, "the trip" complete with luggage, passports, French pastries and Parisian music. I have created the annual erotic Easter egg hunt and had the Mad Hatter to tea on more than one occasion. All this and we have never left home to do it, or needed an American Express card.

One summer, a group of talented friends and I created the *Starlight Cafe* in a friend's huge backyard that had a deck. We made it an old-fashioned coffee house under the stars. We rented tables and chairs for the outdoors, and set up the sound stage on the deck. Some teenage friends offered to be the wait staff, and we made them aprons that said "Starlight Cafe." We also made menus and programs to give out. Every table had flowers that we picked, and a lantern candle. Fresh fruit was placed on all of the tables, as well as teas, coffee and lemonade. Guests could order whatever desserts they wanted to go with their coffee. We charged a small admission to cover the cost of food and the rental so we broke even on expenses. But what a magnificent night we created!

We had everything from a poetry major in college reciting Dylan Thomas poetry, to folk singers, torch singers and every assorted type of musician in between. It was a beautiful star-filled night and by the end of it, everyone was cozily enveloped in the mood, the music and the company. All it took to create it was some organization and planning, desserts, seating, and the willingness of people who had something to share putting it out there.

Needless to say, I am a great supporter and encourager of creating adventures. You would be amazed at the responses you will get and how a few small touches can transform just about anything. I am not talking about throwing big parties either, with huge expense, although a lot of these ideas can translate well for special events, and can be as elaborate as you choose. I am talking about remembering that gleeful child that used to hop out of bed, full of fun and plans for the day, and letting it out of the closet. I am talking about bringing out the explorer in you, the jester, the inventor, the creator, and using your talents to really enhance and enjoy your life.

All of these adventures are adaptable for two or more persons. Everything is laid out, so that the guesswork is eliminated, but open-ended enough for you to add your own personal flair to every occasion.

 *Have fun!*

Play it up and...
send us a postcard,
will you?

Inviting people in

Inviting someone to something, whether it is your home, your place of business, a club, a group, or even into more intimacy, is an important cultural ritual. It sets the tone for the occasion and establishes the degree of comfort we feel. Often it becomes the deciding factor in our willingness to participate in any occasion. We are all familiar with the conventional invitations that pass through our hands during the course of the year—holiday parties, birthdays, anniversaries or New Year's celebrations. But what I am describing, is the seldom exercised skill of consciously making an effort to really draw someone in, to capture their imagination and welcome him or her into a whole new experience. You can create the most fabulous plans and adventures, but you will miss out on so much of the delight and possibility if you don't take the opportunity to properly invite others in to it.

When we feel welcomed, the first thing that usually occurs is a flush of pleasure at being included and acknowledged. Think back to your childhood and receiving that coveted birthday invitation, the phone call for an overnight, and then later on invitations to proms, games, fraternities, and clubs. Early on in our lives, invitations had the ability to delight us (maybe that still happens). So did the response to an occasion that we hosted. Even today, we still want our parties to be special, our invitations coveted, and for everyone to show up, feel relaxed and have a great time.

I remember the first time I invited a boy home for lunch in the fifth grade. Lunch hour was an hour and fifteen minutes, but since I lived close to school, it was a quick walk which left the two of us with an hour to kill. I had saved all of my money and spent every cent of it on a Parker Brothers detective game I thought that he might like to play.

I desperately wanted him to feel happy that he had accepted my invitation. We ate our spaghetti lunch awkwardly, he gave the game a perfunctory glance, and in the end, never showed enough interest to take it out of the box.(Footnote: I saw him twenty years later. He was a zipper salesman in a polyester green suit. He didn't remember me or the game. Not to pass judgment, but girls hang onto your cash.)

When we create an inviting situation, it draws on all our senses. It lures us in.

SCENARIO NO. 1:

Picture a banquet. You enter, having dressed in your finest attire. You are escorted to a magnificently set table where your eyes linger over the presentation, the colors and textures of an exquisitely prepared meal. Your body unconsciously sways seductively to the sound of a saxophone in the distance. You savor the aromas wafting in from the other room. You are heady with anticipation and the tingling delight that the night promises.

SCENARIO NO. 2:

Take yourself to the same banquet. Show up late in your sweats. Slam the door as you enter the room. Kick off your shoes and shout, "Hey, where's the grub?" Before you can notice anything, plug your nose, plug your ears and close your eyes. Now sit down to dinner. How appetizing is this banquet?

When many of us have been in longstanding relationships, or lived with a partner, we take things for granted. We begin to just assume that we go to the movies on Friday or bowling on Sunday. Though it is a great comfort to have a buddy that you can count on to do things with, with so little formality, sometimes we really want to feel special. Many of the complaints we hear stem from feelings of being taken for granted. We miss the courtship courtesies and the attentiveness we showed toward each other when we first met. Look at the huge appeal of romance in the movies and in books. I don't think we all really wish we were involved with Michelle Pfeiffer or Mel Gibson (do we?). I think the appeal is that we all long for passion and that is what these movies and, the characters in them, awaken in us. We want the excitement and the feeling of desirability and attraction that we showed for our lovers when we first met.

The point is that attraction is a full emotional and physical response. It involves our total participation. We love to savor, anticipate and prepare for maximum appreciation. So create a banquet! Use everything you've got to open yourself and each other to the fullest experience possible.

I have a friend who did just that. In a most fabulous fashion, he invited his girlfriend to see *Phantom of the Opera*. He had obtained tickets to give to her as a Christmas gift. The play was not on Christmas day, but he found a way to give her the present on that day anyway. He handed her a large envelope on Christmas morning, one that had smaller envelopes inside. The envelope said, "To be opened on December 28th at 12:00 noon. Please clear the calendar from that time on."

When she opened it, the note said to open all of the clues in the other envelopes in order, and follow the directions exactly. Clue #1 told her to take a leisurely bath, fix her hair and get all dressed up. When she was finished, she was to get in her car and open Clue #2. Clue #2 had her go to the restaurant where they first met (a nice sentimental touch), and ask the maitre'd a riddle. He would know it as the code and give her Clue #3. Clue #3 took her to a favorite music spot where the bartender had her next clue and told her to go to a restaurant around the corner and ask for the hostess. The hostess handed her a card that said, "Look for the gentleman with the red carnation." He was sitting at the table waiting for her and handed her a card which said, *Please join me tonight for dinner and 'Phantom of the Opera.' Your Sweetie.* Just in case someone didn't give her the next instruction, he had also arranged a backup plan with a friend she could call.

He created such excitement, that in both the restaurant and the theatre, everyone heard about it and got involved. They were sure that this was a marriage proposal in the works. Besides the couple, it brought great delight to everyone present. Can you feel the tone and the love with which the night was planned? The anticipation he created? The delight? How do you think his girlfriend felt? Special? Appreciated? Cherished? The tickets alone were a wonderful gift, but look what his style of invitation created for the evening. Can you see the difference it makes?

Invitations can be as elaborate as the above example, or simple, but equally effective. For instance, if you usually go to the movies on a Friday night and then out for pizza, you could simply leave a note on the dashboard of the car and let your partner know how much you love him or her and how much you are looking forward to his or her company.

Enclose a coupon good for "P&C" (popcorn and cuddling).

I once was invited to a man's house for a home-cooked meal and when I got there, he had a roaring fire and a little sign on the dining room table that said *Reserved for Nance.* Boy, did that feel welcoming.

You can write funny messages on a balloon like Being with you is an uplifting experience, I'm walking on air since meeting you, or write a secret message to decode. How about a note left under the pillow? Enclosed in a favorite candy bar? Or attached to the stem of a favorite flower? Try whispering an invitation on the answering machine or voice mail (finally one fun use for voice mail). You can also get ridiculous—a piece of toast with a note that says, Let's toast the town tonight. A sparkling water bottle with a label attached, The thought of this evening has me bubbling with anticipation. How about a coupon for cuddling?

Inviting with finesse also has an added bonus for all of you who are eager to have someone try out one of your favorite sports or hobbies. I'm convinced there are many more activities we would be open to participating in if someone took the time to make it enticing enough. Sometimes that is just the ticket we need to begin to relax our resistance where we would previously have remained rigid.

Here's an example. If you said to me, "Hey, Nance I've got tickets to a baseball game," you would be hard pressed to get me to consider it. You would either have to trap me in a bad bet, drug me with chocolate (known to be very effective), or resort to other fiendish ploys. If, on the other hand, you showed up at my door with a baseball cap and handed me a box of peanuts and Cracker Jacks with a card that said, "You'll have so much fun with me, you may never want to come back!" And then if you pulled out a handmade pennant (pencil and cut paper) that said "Root, root, root for the home team," you would have successfully loosened my resistance, conveying your enthusiasm, delight and desire for me to participate. I would definitely give it

73

a whirl. (I would, however, still stick a large chocolate bar in my pocket).

Manipulative? Not really. More like gentle persuasion. Of course, there are activities and things that are simply not negotiable; we're not remotely interested in, or that are not in our comfort zone. But there are a lot of borderline activities, things we don't break out in hives over, where a welcoming, loving gesture can usually lull us right over the line.

Throughout this book, I will suggest many ideas to go with each event, and you can elaborate by putting on your own personal touches. And then—go wild! Dress up, sing at breakfast, attach a card to the steering wheel, or to a teabag with an invitation for a quiet, relaxing evening. Anything you choose to do will be appreciated. The important thing is that by the time you meet, your guests will be knocking your door down in joyful anticipation.

The At-home
Movie Theatre

THE THEME

I know it's hard to give up paying eight dollars plus
to see a movie, to buy popcorn and a coke for what
it would cost you to fill your tank with gas. And
then there's the thrill of your feet sticking to the
floor where someone's soda spilled. Then you get
to take your seat behind the lady who just
graduated from beauty school with an A+ for her
beehive hairdo. Try leaving that all behind (boo
hoo), and creating your own movie theatre in the
privacy of your home.

There are tickets and movie marquees, and a
concession stand to delight the staunchest of junk
food lovers. Got a whole family of kids? Elaborate
further by turning the evening into a great family
affair or birthday party complete with ushers and
decor. A great hit at a fraction of the cost of going
out to a theatre.

> *When a friend of mine first met my kids,*
> *we were planning on watching the*
> *movie, 'Prince of Tides' at my house. Of*
> *course my kids and I decided to set up a*
> *movie theatre. We took a large piece of*
> *posterboard left over from a project and*
> *the girls drew a big movie marquee of*
> *'Prince of Tides' with pictures on it, and*
> *a caption that said, 'Showing Here*
> *Tonight.' We hung it on the door. We*
> *set up our own theatre with pillows on*
> *the floor. We made a refreshment stand*
> *on the dining room table where we*

had miniature boxes of candy, drinks, bags of handmade popcorn and ice cream bars.

The girls made out a menu with prices from $.01 to $.10. Since they have been around me so much, they took it further. They found a flashlight and a craft's apron with pockets on it, and one of them became the usher while the other one was in charge of the refreshment stand. (Keep in mind that my friend knew nothing about this beforehand.) When he showed up at the door, the usher greeted him and handed him his ticket and money to spend at the concession stand. He was totally surprised and delighted. He proceeded over to the concession stand where he spent some of the money and was informed that he had better spend it all because the stand would be closing shortly (bedtime!) We had a wonderful time. The girls went to sleep and we curled up in our own private theatre.

INVITATION SUGGESTIONS

- ⊠ *Make little admission tickets*

- ⊠ *Cut out a movie review that you send on a card*

- ⊠ *Write up your own review of the movie you plan to see with an admission ticket*

- ⊠ *Keep it a surprise and just invite them over for the evening*

- ⊠ *Coordinate your invitation with the movie, for instance, if it's "Casablanca," you can find a picture of Bogie on a greeting card and write a clever message*

- ⊠ *Send a ticket saying they have won a movie sweepstakes*

RESERVATIONS SUGGESTED

PREPARATION

Choose a movie that you would both like to see and that would be fun for this type of home-viewing scenario. Ask for suggestions if you are not quite sure of what you want to show. Old classic movies are a great choice, especially around the holiday season.

THE ROOM SETUP

You can make a movie poster yourself with pictures or words or maybe pick up an extra poster at the video store. Hang it in the window or doorway where it will first be seen. If you feel really ambitious, you can suspend it over the T.V. Lay out the pillows or comfortable chairs. If the movie has a theme, you can decorate a little bit in that style.

REFRESHMENTS

This is the really fun part.

- *Set up a concession stand with your favorite treats. You can give out play money or tickets for buying things or simply have a sign saying "On the house tonight."*

- *Pop popcorn beforehand and put it in some wonderful popcorn bags or boxes that you find in the party store. Plain brown ones will do fine as well.*

- *You can buy small miniatures of an assortment of candy and chocolates, or if you would like to make some more original snacks than candy and ice cream bars, go for it. How about ice cream sundaes? Fruit platters? Party sandwiches? Cheese or dips with lovely breads and crackers.*

- *You can use the tops of shirt boxes or shoe boxes as carrying trays.*

When you get your snacks, put away the perishables and then proceed to ...

The Main Event

Okay, settle into your places with your snack tray. You can dim all of the house lights and use a flashlight to find your places. Get comfortable in your cozy chairs. Turn on the movie, cuddle up and relax and enjoy.

Family Movie Theatre

This makes a really fun event for the whole family and is a lot less costly than taking everyone to the movies. All of the previous instructions would apply, except you would add more seating and a greater assortment of snacks.

Kids' Movie Theatre

This is great for kids and a particularly welcome activity on rainy days. It is also good for a birthday party.

Invitation Suggestions

⊠ See the Invitation Suggestions at the beginning of this chapter. You might want to send out an invitation to each child with a movie ticket and concession money.

Preparation

See Preparation at the beginning of this chapter and then add to it. Line up pillows or chairs in rows in your house

THE MAIN EVENT

✓ *Have an adult or an older sibling run the concession stand. Give each child a tray for their snacks. Buy miniatures of everything so that everyone has the fun of making their own selection. Have them spend their money.*

✓ *Package fun drinks in spill-proof containers or get small juice boxes in individual sizes.*

✓ *You can add festive touches if it is a birthday party, such as little umbrellas or favors.*

✓ *Flick the lights on and off like in a real theatre and come up and introduce the show.*

✓ *If it's a Disney film and you have any of the plush characters laying around, put them around the theatre. You can use dolls, stuffed animals or posters. For a birthday party, use trinkets from the theme such as key chains or pencils for a goody bag.*

✓ *Keep an usher on hand for bathroom breaks, spills and refills.*

An evening of appreciation and gratitude

THE THEME

Here you are creating an evening to honor someone special, particularly during those occasions and passages where the person could use a little extra acknowledgment or praise.

What would really touch someone and how can you assemble the occasion for different types of relationships? Learn powerful ways to apply this gift specifically to children when they are embarking on some new phase of their lives, like moving away from home, going to college, or beginning a new career.

INVITATION SUGGESTIONS

- ⊠ Create a scroll that says, *Evening Honoring _____ with the date, time and RSVP*

- ⊠ Write a card that says, *How Do I Love Thee, Let's Count the Ways on _____ with the date and time on it*

- ⊠ Buy a small trophy from a party store. Wrap an invitation around it that says, *This is your evening. Join me in utmost gratitude and appreciation ...*

- ⊠ Keep the subject matter a surprise and just send an invitation saying, *I love you. Please meet me at _____*

- ⊠ Design a card out of blank paper and write at least ten things you love about the invitee. Tell them to join you because that's just the tip of the iceberg.

81

Preparation

The first thing I would suggest is to sit down with no interruptions and feel out what you want to communicate to this person. Really spend time feeling who this person is in your life and what they mean to you. This is a lovely experience because, besides the appreciation and gratitude you express to them, you will begin to feel how deeply they have enriched your life.

Ask yourself:
1. *What ways have you been touched by this person?*
2. *What do you really appreciate about them?*
3. *What are your fondest memories together?*
4. *What have been your greatest joys with each other?*
5. *What have you shared together that has really meant a lot to you?*

You can start out by jotting down simple one-liners, I appreciate the way you fix my lunch everyday, the way you take care of the car and keep me safe. Then move on to deeper places of appreciation of what it means to be together. You can write a long letter to them about how you feel or maybe there was some particular incident where they were there for you that you want to thank them for. Move on to your day-to-day life and think of all of the ways that they are there for you that you might not acknowledge too often. Remember the countless reassurances, hugs, words of encouragement, treats, kindnesses offered, shoulder to lean on and the hundreds of other ways that they have been available, open and loving towards you.

Start organizing them in any way you choose. You can write things down on little cards and color-code them if you wish. Memories would be on one color paper and romantic times on another, for instance. Put them in a beautiful basket to be read.

SOME OTHER IDEAS

Make a gratitude list on a long scroll for them to unravel.

Create an appreciation poster, either hand drawn or on a computer. Frame it as a gift It could express gratitude and acknowledgment for being

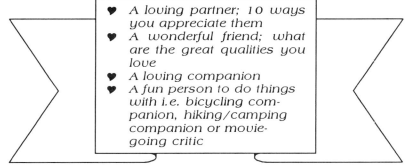

♥ *A loving partner; 10 ways you appreciate them*
♥ *A wonderful friend; what are the great qualities you love*
♥ *A loving companion*
♥ *A fun person to do things with i.e. bicycling companion, hiking/camping companion or movie-going critic*

You get the idea!

DECORATIONS

Decorate the room with all kinds of special mementos. Pull out old photographs or special things that you have around the home that remind you of that person. Take wedding photos out, photos of the birth of your children, special trips, poignant times, anything that you would like to celebrate together that evening. You can also buy a cardboard treasure chest (see Treasure Box in the Gift section) and put all of the cards that you have written about that person in it.

MENU

Choose to make a special meal that the recipient of the evening really loves. How about the things you usually make as treats on birthdays or anniversaries? Tonight would be the night to prepare them. Whatever you decide to serve, make sure your home environment is radiant and lovely. Put beautiful flowers around and use your nicest dishes. Serve everything in a mindful fashion. I like to say grace and give thanks for many blessings over a meal.

You might find the way that feels good for you to express your gratitude.

The Main Event

When the recipient of the occasion arrives, let them know that this is a small token of the appreciation and gratitude that you feel for them in your life. Walk them around the space and show them what you have put up as decorations. Let them know how honored you are to be with them. Share the notes, letters, cards or certificates you have written. I am sure this will bring a floodgate of emotion to the surface and your evening will continue as a heartfelt celebration of love. Share all of the special stories that reflect the best times you have had together and the most wonderful things that have occurred in your relationship together.

Love begets love, and your delight and gratitude will deepen as the evening continues. It is sure to remain one of your fondest and most loving times together.

For Kids

This is a wonderful celebration for your children, especially when they are embarking on a new phase in their lives. Are your children ...
> 1. *Leaving home*
> 2. *Going to college*
> 3. *Traveling abroad*
> 4. *Getting married*
> 5. *Graduating*

Invitation Suggestions

⊠ See previous list at the beginning this chapter.

Preparation

Collect all of the important things that you have saved from their childhood that you think might be appropriate for the occasion — mementos, beautiful drawings, letters that you have shared and school reports. Think back to stories that you want to remember that relate to the evening. Think about your special intimacies and the treasured times you have had together. Plan the whole evening around celebrating and acknowledging them.

DECORATIONS

Follow the same ideas for decorations with photos and mementos of things that would be significant for them.

THE MAIN EVENT

Have the evening unfold in a similar way as the one for Partners. Cook a favorite dinner and invite a best friend to participate and share, or a few friends for that matter. Play the music they love in the background and just let the evening unfold. This is a fabulous sendoff and encouraging boost into the next phase of life.

MATERIALS

- ☐ *An invitation*
- ☐ *Mementos, family pictures, cards*
- ☐ *Art supplies to make posters and posterboard*
- ☐ *Favorite music*

OPTIONAL

- ❤ *Ingredients for a special dinner*
- ❤ *A cardboard treasure chest or something similar*

Pajama Games:
The Pajama Party
(lovely on a cold winter's night or a lazy Sunday)

THE THEME

Would you like a break from being your adult responsible self all the time? Wouldn't it be fun to curl up in your pj's with some Cracker Jacks, cocoa and a good friend? When was the last time you had a pillow fight, played games and giggled? Welcome to a good old-fashioned pajama party. What would you need to create the mood, ambiance and fun that would loosen up your partner? Would your friends or kids enjoy this adventure? Here is a memorable event that will leave you all giggling, cozy, happy and feeling closer. What are you waiting for?

The Lovers' Pajama Party
INVITATION SUGGESTIONS

- ☒ Send a sweet card inviting your lover to join you. Put on the time, place and what the attire is. (Attire can be anything from snuggly pjs, robe, lingerie to pajamas with feet!) Have your partner RSVP and give him/her a meeting place, whether it's your bedroom, den or living room.

- ☒ Write out your invitation on a balloon and hang it in their car or on their chair at breakfast.

- ☒ Attach a note to a cuddly stuffed animal you might have hanging around, or buy a small cuddly creature and attach the invitation to it. You can even get fancy and mail it.

✉ *Write a love poem as an invitation.*

✉ *Attach a note to a set of playing cards, a game or book saying, Spend the evening playing or reading with me.*

✉ *Mail or attach your partner's invitation to a gift of some sexy undergarments if you have decided the attire for the evening will be lingerie.*

✉ *Leave a note on your partner's pillow.*

Please join me for fun & frolic at the First Annual Pajama Party for Lovers!

Time: 8:00 P.M.
Place: Master bedroom
100 Oak Street, Your Town.

RSVP by Wed, October 3rd.
Clothing: Robes, snuggly pj's, ponytail, etc.
☆ ☆ ☆ ☆ ☆
P.S. You can bring your favorite stuffed animal.
☆ ☆ ☆ ☆ ☆

PREPARATION

♥ *Set the room up exactly the way you like it. I suggest you clean the room thoroughly (Boo! okay but it's worth it). Pile it full of pillows. You can make a little cocoon, nest or fort for yourself like you did when you were a kid. Set the books up in one corner of the room or you can create a little reading corner. I remember the fun of hanging up sheets everywhere trying to design little private forts for myself.*

💜 *It would be fun to have lots of books around to choose from. You can choose your favorite books and magazines to read, or go the kid's route and scrounge up your old-time favorite fairy tales. If you don't own any old favorites, go to the library and browse through the children's section.*

💜 *Besides the old classics, you might find some interesting new books that weren't around yet when you were a child.*

💜 *Find or borrow some favorite games from childhood such as Monopoly, Clue, Chutes and Ladders, Scrabble, card games, jacks, or anything else you enjoy. Collect pillows of all assorted shapes and sizes.*

MENU

Snacks for this evening can be pretty casual, something that you might have had at a pajama party when you were a kid, or that you particularly love and don't usually give yourself permission to eat. How about hot chocolate with mini marshmallows, puddings, fruits (remember those orange slices you would put in your mouth and smile with?), your favorite cookies, nuts, or dips? (You can even go as far as Ding Dongs although I'll never admit to suggesting it). Except for the hot drinks, get everything set up on the tray beforehand so it is ready to go.

THE MAIN EVENT

Okay, your lover is going to be here in a few minutes.

💜 *Get into your pj's and bring all of your old teddy bears, stuffed animals or anything else you might like to have decorating the room. If you really want to go at it, you can even have them holding books or playing games.*

♥ *Invite your partner into the room. You can have reading lamps off in the corner and begin your evening. Share snacks, read stories to each other, play games, have a pillow fight, reawaken the child in you. Tell stories about your childhood to each other, (not the horror ones you have probably already shared, but about what it was like growing up for you). What were your favorite childhood movies? What books did you love? Hopefully you have brought some of those books in for the evening. Who were your best friends? What pranks did you play? Did you have sleepovers? A treehouse? What helped you through your childhood? What were your most special times? What are your best memories growing up? Share something about that part of yourself. Not in the mood for talking? Play marbles, jacks or favorite games with each other.*

♥ *You so often see each other as your adult responsible self. It's so nice to be able to connect to the other places that awaken your spirit. It also gives you a different appreciation for your partner, and allows you to see a much more tender, vulnerable and playful person that might be missing in your day-to-day lives.*

KIDS' PAJAMA PARTY
Run through the main ideas so you get a feeling for the evening.

INVITATION SUGGESTIONS

★ *Send an invitation to your child and perhaps to their favorite doll or stuffed animal as well*

★ *Deliver a balloon invitation for each child*

★ *Mail out cards to your children (kids love to get cards, and enclose one miniature for their favorite loved one)*

★ *Attach an invitation to a favorite candy bar*

PREPARATION

Wherever you are setting this party up, make sure it remains a surprise. Therefore, it should be in a room that you can close off. For younger children, set up the room with a reading corner, lots of pillows, favorite books, games, puzzles, crayons, paper and some fun music. Also include lots of pillows for pillow fights. Dress in your pj's and have them meet you or take them to the room. You can have a big sign on the door with your names and the party. For instance, the sign could say:

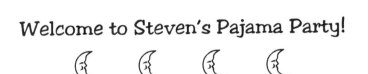

Welcome to Steven's Pajama Party!

THE MAIN EVENT

Kids so rarely get to see you being playful that they will love this evening. Kick off your slippers, read them your old stories and tell them your favorite stories about growing up. If you have any photos of yourself as a child, pull them out. Kids love to see what you looked like. Who were your best friends? What were your favorite games? Why not teach them your favorites and learn some of theirs? This can be a really magical night of sharing.

MATERIALS

Please look to the end of this chapter for a complete list of materials.

FOR OLDER KIDS

What a nice way to relax together. You can set up the room in a really cozy way, and you may want to add a few other touches. Do you feel like painting toenails tonight? Playing with usually forbidden makeup? Playing cards? Listening to your favorite music? Dancing? Playing chess, Monopoly, Clue or Scrabble.

Make snacks that are a special treat, maybe even the ones you give out on birthdays. This is a great way to connect and communicate, especially as schedules and changing concerns can erode some of your communication and intimacy together.

This is so much fun! (And on my repeat list of adventures for the near future.) Invite a group of friends to spend the evening and even to a sleepover.

INVITATION SUGGESTIONS

Read the section on Invitations in The Lover's Pajama Party and choose one you would like. Or, you can do one for the whole office gang by writing a funny memo. Include on the invitation the attire as well as instructions to bring something fun that reminds them of their childhood. Have everyone wear pj's or a bathrobe. You can each bring a story you loved, a game you want to play, an instrument if you play one, your yearbook, or photos of yourself when you were little.

PREPARATION

Read Preparation in The Lover's Pajama Party for suggestions. You would add more reading lamps, lots of big pillows and ask everyone to bring their own pillow for a pillow fight.

MENU

As far as the snacks go, read through the Menu section on The Lover's Pajama Party. If it's a large crowd, have everyone bring their favorite treat and the host or hostess can provide hot chocolate or sodas, tea and juice.

THE MAIN EVENT

See The Main Event for the Lover's Pajama Party and add one or more of the following.

ACTIVITY SUGGESTIONS

* *Share your best childhood memories*
* *Tell unusual stories of friendship and adventure*
* *Describe what helped you survive difficult times*
* *Remember wonderful stories of pets*
* *Play broken telephone*
* *Sing some favorite old songs*
* *Create elaborate forts to play in. Divide in groups and let everyone choose from a pile of materials.*
* *Tell ghost stories and schedule the pillow fight*
* *Hand out prizes for the best fort creation*

93

✳ *Have art supplies, paint, crayons, scissors, stickers, rubber stamps and papers to play with*

✳ *Do a talent show, paper bag dramatics or play charades*

✳ *Or you can leave it to everyone to play, hang out, talk, have snacks.*

This is great either as a co-ed or a same sex evening.

MATERIALS (SUITABLE FOR ALL PAJAMA PARTIES)

♥ *A selection of books to read*
♥ *A selection of favorite games*
♥ *Pillows in all shapes and sizes*
♥ *Favorite snacks*
♥ *Photo album of yourself as a kid*
♥ *Instrument, if you play one*
♥ *Materials to make a fort*
♥ *Art supplies*
♥ *Prizes for the best creation*

Florence Nightingale Day

THE THEME

Dear Ann Landers,
Help! The car needs new brakes, the dog just threw up on the carpet, my computer is down with a deadline tomorrow, and my kid is quarantined with the chicken pox (the only major childhood disease I've missed). My parents have sold their house and are moving in with us next month. They both require special diets. I better dash this off now since my car is in the shop and I will need to jog the two miles to the post office so I can send this before dark.

Signed 'Calgon, Take Me Away'

This person could use some pampering! Here is the answer to his/her prayers— an entire celebratory day appropriate for all of us, but a gift to those tireless care givers in your life.

INVITATION SUGGESTIONS

- ☒ *Write a Congratulations Letter for a mini vacation day that they have won*

- ☒ *Invite them to be Queen or King for the Day. Enclose a crown*

- ☒ *Tie up a box of bonbons, wrapped in whatever magazine the person loves, inviting them out for the day*

- ☒ *Leave a pack of bubble bath with a note that says, You'll get a long leisurely period to enjoy this as well as lots more relaxation time. I'm taking you away!*

95

⊠ *Send them a card telling them how much you appreciate their efforts and how this day is set aside just for them*

⊠ *Write them an Ann Landers letter about their life and then send them her response saying, This person could really use a break, and here it is!*

⊠ *Hand them a book of coupons redeemable for everything you have planned. Example, Good for one limousine ride, one massage, one dinner out — all to be redeemed immediately.*

PREPARATION

You are inviting this person to totally relax and be taken care of for the day. That means that you have handled everything in your own personal schedule as well as theirs that could possibly derail the day. Make sure you have arranged for childcare or work replacement so that your time is totally flexible. Food shopping, kid's lunches, carpool, emergencies, after-school care, you name it! Check their calendar to make sure the day chosen does not have any appointments: dentist, doctor, hair or veterinarian. (If you are a Californian, no astrologers, psychics, therapists or body workers appointments. No reservations for a hot tub at the spa). In other words, clear the decks.

If you are keeping the day a surprise, find out as discreetly as possible what they would love to do. If you are planning something that is weather dependent, make sure you have a backup plan in case of rain, sleet or snow. Go to the library and pick up some books by their favorite authors or buy magazines they love.

To add a little something extra, pick up some treats or special snacks. If you are arranging a visit that will include a treasured friend of theirs, make arrangements well in advance. The real enjoyment of the day is for the recipient not to have to handle one single detail.

Make a cardboard sign for the car that says So and so's private limousine for the day. Make sure that you have cleaned the limo, let them sit in the backseat and be driven around. Get them out of the house before they can do one chore.

The Main Event

Start the day by making a beautiful tray with their favorite foods. Drop it off and leave them to have quiet time. If the day's activities will be their choice, ask them what they would most like to do. In case they are too stunned to reply, have a few suggestions ready. Perhaps they would like to take a walk on the beach, sit in the library and read, visit a friend, or go shopping. Maybe their idea of heaven is a leisurely bath, sitting in front of the fireplace or browsing through a favorite bookstore. Maybe they would like to play golf, swim or take a hike in the woods, followed by tea at a favorite spot.

The idea is that it is their day; you chauffeur them, get out of the way, and pick them up whenever they ask. You can have a picnic lunch packed with foods they enjoy, or give them money for a lovely lunch out if they are choosing to go shopping or spend time in the city.

More Elaborate and Expensive

$ *Get them a gift certificate for a massage. Make sure it is with somebody they would be comfortable with so they can fully relax*

$ *Schedule a hot tub time and pack them a towel, shampoo and a change of clothes*

$ *Reserve and pay for a haircut, a manicure, a pedicure, or a facial*

$ *Schedule an hour with a personal trainer at a gym*

$ *Plan an afternoon at the movies. Cut out the listings, buy them a ticket, buy some popcorn or their favorite movie snack, drop them off and pick them up*

$ *Buy a ticket to a matinee theatre performance they have been longing to see*

$ *Arrange a surprise visit with an old friend or buddy that they rarely have time to be with. Set up a reservation at a restaurant they might like to go to together. Drop them off and pick them up when they are finished. Handle the bill by credit card or by phone arrangement so that they don't have to deal with it*

$ *Have an invitation waiting for them at the end of the day to join you for dinner, or dinner and dancing. Handle all of the reservations*

$ *Send them to the city with an envelope of money to buy something wonderful and frivolous just for themselves which they ordinarily would never think of doing*

Write them a note and hand it to them at the end of the day. Tell them how much you appreciate their ongoing efforts in your life. Do you know how good it will feel to them to be acknowledged. It will change their whole outlook, and yours too!

Schedule their next Florence Nightingale celebration day and don't wait so long next time!

MATERIALS

1. *A clear and free day*

2. *Transportation*

3. *The fixings for a picnic or lunch money*

4. *Cardboard sign for your limousine service*

MATERIALS (NICE EXTRAS)

- ✓ *Movie tickets with popcorn and refreshments*
- ✓ *Theatre tickets*
- ✓ *Massage or personal care gift such as haircut, manicure, pedicure or facial*
- ✓ *Dinner reservations or delicious homemade meal*
- ✓ *Pocket money (As my dad would say)*

The key to the success of this day is that every arrangement, detail and facet of it, is taken care of totally.

An Evening in Paris

THE THEME

Who wouldn't love to invite their lover to Paris if they thought they could? Here is your opportunity for that perfect romantic trip you dreamed of— a fantasy adventure for lovers. What does one wear for a stroll down the Champs Élysées? What are the most exciting invitations to send? Where do you get the proper passport? How do you set up a delicious crèperie? A stunning bistro? Make beautiful music? Here is everything you need to make it an unforgettable trip without using up one bonus mile, maxing out your credit card or getting jet lag.

This is the kind of adventure that works wonderfully for lovers, but you might also like to invite your friends or perhaps your children on your next trip. What do you need to add for friends that makes it a great evening? How do you set up the plane ride for kids, the trip through customs and a great evening of activities?

PARIS FOR LOVERS

I originally created this event as a surprise in a workshop that I put on about creating adventures. It was the last activity of the day. I had created a master passport by copying the outline of mine at the copy shop on heavy card stock. At the break, I handed everyone their passports and told them they were on their way to Paris. Then I led them to the hidden Parisian café in the room behind a curtained partition I had created.

I had signs posted and framed that said *Café du Paris* on them. I had hung swag curtains over the windows and filled the ledges with baskets of flowers. All of the tables were covered with white tablecloths. A friend had some beautiful dishes, that said *Café Paris* on them, which we set the tables with. Bouquets of daisies decorated each table, with small *Réservé* cards at each place setting for the guests. To greet them, Edith Piaf was singing on the CD.

We served French pastries, biscuits and raspberries soaked in liqueur in cut orange halves. Colorful books loaned from the library of the Louvre and Paris were placed throughout the room.

There was something so magical about creating the very things we had been talking about in the workshop. When people entered the café, they were astonished. A few of them had tears in their eyes from the sheer impact and delight of the surprise, and they were amazed at how real it felt in terms of being transported someplace different.

We had a ball. One of the women in the group was a singer, and unbeknownst to all of us, another woman spoke French fluently. We set up an impromptu performance. After a beautiful introduction in French, the singer came out and performed. The day culminated in a brilliant, beautiful and heartfelt ending. We parted with promises to create another adventure soon!

INVITATION SUGGESTIONS

Have some fun with this one. Haven't you always dreamed of inviting someone to Paris with you? Well, here's your chance. Two weeks before the date:

> ☒ *Send a telegram or registered letter informing them that they have won an evening in Paris*

> ☒ *Invite them as your lover to the most romantic city on earth. Make a card with the Eiffel Tower on it or with pictures of people kissing*

⊠ *Send a note with an invitation and have the whole thing be in French. Include an RSVP*

⊠ *Enclose a passport either with the invitation or after they RSVP and say they can make it. It works great if you take your own passport to a copy shop and reproduce it on heavy stock paper. Then put a picture of the person on the inside with anything else that you like*

⊠ *Send postcards from Paris. Pick up the closest foreign-looking card you can find and write, Wish you were here, can't wait to see you, or Counting the minutes 'til we are together*

⊠ *Send a little something in the mail that's for the trip, like a beret or a scarf or something sexy to wear*

⊠ *Buy a dictionary with popular French phrases in it*

PREPARATION

The event is so much fun to create. There are a million ways to set it up that will make it an extraordinary evening.

DECORATIONS

Well, let's start with some great ideas.

✓ *Go to the library and take out some beautiful art books on the Louvre or the Musée d'Orsay and place them around the room. You can also take out books with lush photographs of Paris.*

✓ *Some airlines or travel agents will have posters on Paris that they might be willing to part with, or you can color-Xerox anything that you particularly love. Arrange the inside of your house beautifully. If you have a deck or a nice outdoor space, you can also set up a bistro outside under the stars. (Realize that any space will do, even a studio apartment. I've created Paris in a small room and it looked spectacular.)*

✓ *Take a small round table if you have one, or if not, use a regular table and cover it with a tablecloth, either white or any color you choose. For a large table, use a basket of flowers; or on a small round one, place a few flowers in a vase. Put a little sign on the table that says Reservé and set the table with some beautiful glasses and a bottle of French wine, or perhaps a sparkling nonalcoholic French cider. You could either buy or borrow some type of French music—anything from Edith Piaf to Jacques Brel or cabaret songs. Libraries frequently have music on hand that can be borrowed. Ask your librarian for help in making your selection.*

✓ *To get more elaborate, you could create a menu and leave it on the table with the evening's fare on it. A nice bottle of French perfume for her or cologne for him, elegantly wrapped at their place is a great touch.*

PACKING A BAG

A fun thing to do is pack a little overnight bag and leave it by the door with something wonderful for your partner to wear. How about something silky and sexy or maybe just a black turtleneck. If you want to look authentic (although this is not my personal taste), you can have a phoney pack of cigarettes, chocolate or bubble gum flavored.

MENU

Paris evokes the image of world class cuisine. We think of French wines, fresh bread and cheese, great chefs, fresh produce, and crèpes. If you walked down the streets of Paris, you would be greeted on a regular basis by small, inexpensive crèpe stands. You can choose crèpes filled with jams, butter and sugar and fresh fruits. It is a delightful experience, and not too difficult to recreate at home.

One time I created a crèperie for my *Evening in Paris*. I cut a window out of a large piece of posterboard and hung it up in the pass through between the kitchen and the dining room. (You can actually hang it up anywhere.) I decorated it by painting in large letters, *Crèpe Bretonne*. Then I strung twinkling Christmas lights all around it for a festive effect. I drew a menu for the evening's crèpe offerings and posted it on the wall. Donning a beret, my best French accent (a remnant from my childhood in Montreal), and an apron (the only time you'd ever get me to wear one), I invited my guests to the window to order their crèpes. For some great crèpe choices, and other delicious French treats, see the recipes at the end of this chapter.

THE MAIN EVENT

Okay, the place looks beautiful, the music is on in the background and your lover arrives at the appointed hour. Let the fun begin.

- ✓ *Greet them at the door in your best French accent. Escort them to the table.*

- ✓ *Listen to the beautiful music. Have a little tête à tête or night of intimate conversation. Dance to the music.*

- ✓ *Serve a simple or extravagant dinner to enjoy. Of course, the more delicious the meal or the more sumptuous the delicacies, the more the evening is enhanced. But, dinner can also be as simple as a salad Niçoise and some good French bread, plus wine or cider. Or a simple onion soup and filled crèpes. You could make a platter of hors d'oeuvres like mushrooms and melted brie on French bread or even a lovely French pastry served with coffee. We have provided a few great recipes here for your dining pleasure and the library is full of great cookbooks if you want to get elaborate and do a Duck à l'orange or create some other famous French cuisine for the evening.*

✓ Take out travel posters of places that you have visited, or wish to, and share them.

✓ Put on your French costumes and take photos of your evening. Speak with French accents. Give each other a pet French name for the evening.

✓ Rent a wonderful French movie with English subtitles.

✓ Keep an album of all your travel adventures.

PARIS FOR FRIENDS

Read over the basic instructions for planning Paris for Lovers so that you can get a basic feel for the evening. Then you can adapt it or change what you want that would make it fun for a group of friends. Obviously, the mood and tone of the evening would be different, but the setting and decorations might stay the same.

INVITATION SUGGESTIONS

You can invite people in basically the same fashion as Paris for Lovers, or put together a tour inviting them to a certain place in Paris, such as the Moulin Rouge, for the evening.

✈ Suggest attire ideas, such as everyone wearing a black or red beret, or anything they might have from their own trips to France. You can also ask people to bring photos, postcards or slides of a Parisian trip if you like.

✈ If you'd like to make the evening more of a planned adventure, you can have a lot of fun setting the stage for it. In your invitation, give everyone a character to play, and arrive as that character for the evening. It could be as simple as a French man named Louis, or a historical character such as Napoleon, or a creative type, such as Toulouse-Lautrec or Jacques Brel. You can also choose a time in French history and have people try on their own fantasy characters.

106

✦ *Think about the guests that are being invited—who are they? Are they lovers of music, art or history? Try to assign your guests a role they would love to play. Then everyone who comes to the party can bring their own special props and costumes.*

PREPARATION

Preparations can be the same as for the *Evening for Lovers*, except you would want to set up a few more tables and arrange a menu suitable for larger crowds.

MENU

See Menu under Paris for Lovers. You can print up the evening's fare for each table, which is always fun. Ask a friend or two to be the servers. If you want it to be a potluck, everyone can pitch in for the meal and make it a combined affair by bringing their favorite breads, cheeses, French soups, salads or a rich dessert. You can also set up a crèpe stand, as I mentioned previously, and serve crèpes as the main course (if there are not too many people), or as a lovely dessert. Let the good company and the good food flow. There are also some classic French movies with English subtitles you might like to enjoy with your coffee and dessert, such as *Cousin, Cousine*.

THE MAIN EVENT

Okay, play with this one.

✓ *You can set up a dinner cabaret, and if you have a few entertainers in the group, invite people to perform. If they're in costume, it's a good chance to be an exhibitionist. You can also have each person do five minutes of performing in the character that they came as. For instance, if you were Toulouse Lautrec, you can come with paints, and include everyone in a painting experience. Or the artist could talk to people about his or her life as a creative person. You can have a jar set*

107

out with names, such as Marie Antoinette or Maurice Chevalier and settings, such as the French Revolution or Paris in the 40's. Your guests can pick one out of the jar. Their whole table can get in the mood and create a small scenario to perform, all in character.

✓ Or, you can simply put on cabaret music, eat, relax, dance and have a wonderful time. Take lots of photos.

✓ Some people make these celebrations a quarterly ritual. I met a woman at the hair salon one day who was having some type of elaborate *do* done. When I inquired, she said it was for her Evita party. Every few months, a whole group of friends got together around an adventure theme and planned a party. It was always a huge success.

✓ Every year has its doldrums times—after the Christmas season, a long rainy spell or tax season. What a wonderful idea to create different adventures during these times or on any special occasion. Someone different can host it, and you will find that you can have wonderful occasions to look forward to all year round.

PARIS FOR KIDS

This is a wonderful idea as an adventure for kids. You can combine this with the Paris for Friends event where children are included. Look over the Paris for Lovers section to see what elements of decor and food you would like to use. Since children love to play and pretend, I've included an array of activities and suggestions that would be particularly exciting to them and make it an unforgettable evening.

INVITATION SUGGESTIONS

Look over the suggestions in Paris for Lovers. There are lots of fun ideas that will adapt well for kids. For example, sending a passport, a postcard or a telegram.

PREPARATION

Look through Preparations in Paris for Lovers to decide which ambiance you want to create. Then I would add some or perhaps all of these great extras.

- ✓ *Have them pack a small suitcase with a few favorite belongings*
- ✓ *Take their pictures with a Polaroid to glue into a passport.*

MENU

Look under Menu in Paris for Lovers for suggestions. The crèperie would be wonderful for kids. Kids love crèpes especially when they get to order them up by themselves, just like ice cream sundaes with toppings. Appoint one of the kids as the server. If crèpes seem too difficult, how about French rolls and cheese, croissants or finger foods? Let them order in French from the menu. (Be gracious and accept all accents.) Let them pay for the crèpes with their French francs or play money. Serve them sparkling drinks in special glasses or wine glasses for the occasion.

THE MAIN EVENT

Look through The Main Event in Paris for Lovers and Paris for Friends, then add these extras.

- ✓ *Give the kids plane tickets and set up an area outside or away from the main event as an airplane to take them to Paris.*

- ✓ *Set out cushions and give out little bags of nuts, pretzels and drinks. Have someone be the flight attendant. Let them know when you are about to land and then take them off the plane.*

- ✓ *Hand them their passports. Have some area be the customs area where they pass through to go to Paris. Stamp their passports with rubber stamps.*

- ✓ *Set up some easels and paints and let them be artists on the left bank of Paris.*

- ✓ *Create an art corner with paper and crayons available for the younger ones.*

- ✓ *Rent a travel movie of Paris to show them the major highlights of the city.*

- ✓ *Give them French spending money and set up a little souvenir stand with postcards and a few trinkets to buy.*

MATERIALS

For main Materials, see Paris for Lovers. In addition, you can add:

- ★ *An easel set up with watercolors, or paper and crayons*

- ★ *Plane tickets*

- ★ *Francs or play money*

- ★ *Passports (Polaroid camera, if you have one to take pictures)*

- ★ *Souvenirs for the stand*

RECIPES

Basic Crèpes

1 cup all-purpose flour	3 eggs
3/4 cup water	2 Tbs. salad oil
2/3 cup milk	1/4 tsp. salt

1. In a blender of food processor, combine all ingredients. Process until batter is smooth, stopping moter once or twice to scrape flour from sides of container.
2. Cover and refrigerate batter for at least 1 hour. Blend batter well before making crepes.
3. Make crepes using a lightly oiled 6-inch pan. Stack them as each crepe is completed.
Makes 16 to 20 crepes.

Seafood Crèpes

1 lb. rock cod or sea bass fillets	2 Tbs. butter
All-purpose flour	3 green onions, thinly sliced

Pinch each white pepper, ground nutmeg and cayenne pepper
2 cups (½ lb.) shredded Gruyere or Swiss cheese

1 cup milk	1/2 lb. Bag small shrimp

½ cup chicken broth, homemade or canned

1 Tbs. dry vermouth	½ cup shredded Parmesan cheese

Buckwheat Crèpes (recipe follows)

1. Place fish fillets on rack above ½ inch of water in medium frying pan. Bring water to boil, cover, reduce heat, and steam until fish looks opaque and flakes when tested with a fork (6 - 8 min.). Drain and cool. Remove and discard bones and skin. Separate fish into flakes. (You should have about 2 cups.)
2.Mix flaked fish, green onions, 1 cup of the Gruyere cheese, and about half of the shrimp. Fill crèpes, dividing seafood mixture evenly, and roll them up. Place side by side in a shallow buttered baking dish 9 x 13 inches.
3. For sauce, melt butter in saucepan over medium heat. Stir in flour, pepper, nutmeg, and cayenne; cook until bubbling. Remove from heat and mix in milk and chicken broth. Cook, stirring constantly, until thickened and bubbling. Stir in remaining 1 cup Gruyere cheese until melted; fold in remaining shrimp and vermouth. Pour cheese and shrimp sauce over crepes; sprinkle with Parmesan cheese. (If made ahead, cover and refrigerate.)
4. Bake, uncovered, in a 400 F oven until crepes are heated through and cheese sauce is lightly browned (20 - 30 minutes).
Makes 8 servings.

Recipes...

Buckwheat Crêpes

In blender or food processor, combine 3/4 cup plus 2 Tbs. all-purpose flour, 2 Tbs. buckwheat flour, 3/4 cup water, 2/3 cup milk, 3 eggs, 2 Tbs. salad oil, and 1/4 tsp. salt. Process for about 1 minute at high speed; scrape down any flour clinging to sides, then process again briefly.

Cover and refrigerate batter at least 1 hour. Makes six or seven inch crepes, stack as each crepe is completed.

Makes 16 - 20 crepes.

Orange-Dessert Crêpes

1 cup all-purpose flour	1/2 tsp. vanilla
2 Tbs. powdered sugar	1/4 tsp. Salt
3/4 cup water	Orange Butter (recipes follows)
2/3 cup milk	

1/2cup orange-flavored liqueur (opt.) or whipped cream
3 eggs   2 Tbs. salad oil

1. In blender or food processor, combine flour, powdered sugar, water, milk, eggs, oil, vanilla, and salt. Process until batter is smooth, stopping once or twice to stir flour from sides of container. Cover and refrigerate batter for 1 hour.

2. Blend batter well before making crèpes, then make crepes using a lightly oiled 6- to 7-inch pan. Stack each crèpe as completed. If made ahead, place in a shallow pan, cover lightly with foil, and reheat in a 250° F oven until crèpes are warmed through (about 15 minutes).

3. To serve, spoon some orange butter onto half of each crèpe, using a scant tablespoon for each; fold crèpes in quarters and arrange, slightly overlapping, on a warm, rimmed, heatproof platter.

4. Flame the crèpes by heating liqueur in a small metal pan until barely warm to touch. (Liqueur will not flame if overheated.) Ignite carefully and pour over crèpes. Lift crepes with 2 forks until flames die out. If you do not flame the crèpes, serve crepes with whipped cream.

Makes 6 servings.

AND MORE RECIPES

Orange Butter

In a medium bowl, beat ½ cup butter until fluffy.
Gradually beat in ½ cup sugar, then blend in grated rind of
1 orange. Adding about 2 teaspoons at a time, gradually
beat in 3 tablespoons orange juice.
(If made ahead, cover and refrigerate; let stand at room
temperature at least 1 hour before serving).

Makes about 1 cup.

Salad Niçoise

The marinated vegetables, which are the basis of this southern
French dish, can be served as they are, or can be tossed with
greens.
4 Tbs. combined lemon juice and wine vinegar
2 cups cooked green beans, cut in 1-inch lengths (warm or
cold)
1/2 cup olive oil
1 tomato, cut in bite-size pieces   1/2 tsp. Salt
2 Tbs. Capers (or more to taste)   1 tsp. dried chervil
8 or more olives
2 cups sliced cooked potatoes (warm or cold)
4 to 6 cups soft greens (optional)
Pepper
Tuna (optional)
1. Make a dressing of lemon juice, vinegar, oil, salt, chervil,
and generous amounts of pepper, and toss with all the
ingredients except the greens in a deep serving bowl. This
can be prepared in advance or just before serving, whichever
is most convenient.
2. Just before serving, mix in greens.

Makes 4 servings.

Don Ho, move over ...
a night in the Hawaiian islands

THE THEME

Create a tropical paradise in the middle of a Michigan blizzard. Here is the perfect pickup for those mid-winter weather blahs. You'll be singing Elvis Presley tunes (OK, that's optional) while you put this luau together. Where do you get grass skirts (and why?), find great costumes, scenery and props? Turn your home into a warm, breezy beach. Get out your juice squeezer and set up your own tropical bar. There are enough ideas to keep you and your friends "limbo-ing" the night away; everything you need for either a shipwrecked crowd of two or the whole office gang.

INVITATION SUGGESTIONS

- ✉ *Cut out suns of colored paper and write out an invitation on the back.*
- ✉ *Send a small sample package of suntan lotion with an invitation wrapped around it.*
- ✉ *Send or hand out a tropical drink with an invitation wrapped around it.*

115

⊠ *Enclose those small tropical drink umbrellas with an invitation.*

⊠ *Put a dress code on the invitation. You can request summer attire, bathing suits or shorts and T's, or Hawaiian shirts and sunglasses. Put an RSVP with a BYOS (Bring Your Own Sun toys, Suntan lotion and Sunglasses), but keep the party a surprise.*

⊠ *Make up a Free Trip Certificate by hand or on the computer and send one out to all your guests.*

⊠ *Go crazy! Make your own Hawaiian music tape informing your guests they have won a trip to the Islands. Send a Winning Trip Invitation to all the guests to bring with them.*

PREPARATION

With this one, you can go wild and have a ball. You can create with as much hoopla and fanfare as you like. Some ideas:

DECORATIONS
The Tropical Beach:

✿ *Buy kids' small inflatable wading pools (especially when they are off season and on clearance) and blow them up. Cover the floor or carpet with a big blue tarp that you can easily buy at a hardware store. That way it will keep the sand off the floor and also look like the ocean. You can have one or more of these if your party space is large. Fill the pools with either sand or colored water (you can put in a few drops of blue food coloring). You can place the pools outside if it's not too cold. Have an assortment of sand toys on hand. Shovel, pails and scoopers work well as do all kinds of seashells or pebbles you might have gathered. (Next summer, put a bag away for future adventures.)*

✿ On the blue tarp, cut out fish in all shapes and sizes or buy them from a party store. Hang up one or two large suns that you either buy at a party store or you can make yourself out of yellow posterboard. You can also buy large tissue and cardboard palm trees, parrots, and assorted tropical theme items. Prop up the tree and hang the birds from the ceiling. In a pinch, you can make all of this but it is quite inexpensive to buy and infinitely easier than spending your time wrestling with six feet of posterboard. (Spend the money!)

✿ At my local party store, the decorations run only a couple of dollars each. You can also buy plastic crabs and fish. Grass skirts are available for about $5.00 each and you can purchase leis for $1.00 each. Have a big box of leis at the door for people to wear and some extra sunglasses. A few grass skirts are a great extra to offer your less inhibited friends, and provide some straw hats for the shyer ones in the crowd (who don't feel like exposing their privates in company).

✿ You can turn on all the lights for a bright sunny effect, but I prefer to use strings of Christmas lights which can be wound around the fake palm trees, or up around the ceiling. If you have a long stick, set up a limbo contest area, or use a broom for the limbo stick (finally, a fun use for a broom). Lay a few beach towels and beach chairs around.

✿ For music, get some tapes that are just the sounds of the ocean in the background, or if you want dancing music, ask your local music store for suggestions. There is a lot of Hawaiian music available (frequently on clearance). Turn up the heat for a tropical setting and set a few fans to blow breezes around the room.

REFRESHMENTS — FUN! FUN! FUN!

The (tropical) sky is the limit!

- *Let's start with drinks. You can concoct tropical punches out of pineapple juices, sparkling sodas and wine coolers. Make a batch of non-alcoholic or alcoholic piña coladas and add those little tropical umbrellas. You can even set up a small area with a sign and have someone tend bar. Call it whatever you like, how about The Tropicana, The Summer Squeeze, The Main Squeeze, or The Tropic Teasers. Collect lots of swizzle sticks, umbrellas and decorations for the drinks.*

- *You can prepare anything from finger food to a simple or elaborate barbecue. Halve pineapples, scoop them out and fill them with fresh fruit. Get some fresh coconut if it's available or use some shredded unsweetened dry coconut. Mini pizzas, egg rolls, peanut noodles, and salads all make great finger food. So do salsas and chips and cold seafood.*

- *For a barbecue, you can serve grilled fish with fruit salsas or barbecued ribs, chicken, kabobs, or burgers. For the non-meat eaters, veggie kabobs or grilled vegetables are delicious.*

- *For desserts, try key lime pies, coconut cookies, coconut cakes, or toast marshmallows on sticks over the barbecue, (you can even do it in the fireplace.) These are just a few ideas to get you going, but use your imagination.*

THE MAIN EVENT

Greet your guests and invite them into your tropical paradise.

✿ *You can stop at the bar for a drink before you sit down and mingle. Dip your toes in the pool or sand box. Set up an area for card playing. Put on some great dancing or hula music.*

✿ *Have friends bring over guitars and instruments for a sing-along around the beach fire. It could be in front of a fireplace or around the pool. Have a seashell hunt for hidden seashells around the house or build a sand castle. Reward the winner.*

✿ *Have a best tropical costume contest.*

✿ *Have a limbo contest.*

✿ *Enjoy a beach barbecue.*

✿ *Show the video "South Pacific" at the end of the evening!*

✿ *Feeling flush (or reckless?) Hire a steel drum band for dancing!*

Section
Four

Stoking the Flames... evenings for lovers

It is so easy to be overwhelmed by the laundry list of tasks and responsibilities we face each day. Usually, we spend our leisure time with our lovers doing the same old thing: gutter cleaning, buying Clorox at Costco, doing chores, and digging coffee grounds out of the garbage disposal.

When asked if we have the time, energy or inclination to add one more *should*, even a romantic one, to the equation, most of us would hightail it out of here before we hear one further word of instruction, feigning exhaustion. But just take a moment out and give some thought to what you spend your time on now. How much of it gets eaten up doing errands? On the telephone? Or in front of the T.V.? Now honestly answer this question (before you hightail it out of here), how much time do you spend developing and deepening your relationship with your lover? How much spontaneity, joy and playfulness do you express to each other on a daily basis? Yet, it is our intimacies which feed and nourish our souls and give our lives a sense of deep purpose and meaning.

Most people, when asked to remember really intimate occasions with their partners, will usually say something to the effect of, When we first got married or When we first started dating or Before our children were born ... as if these occasions were only to be done as a courting ritual or at the beginning of a relationship. Granted, the first flush of excitement and the initial carefree stage has developed into a life full of the challenges of intimacy and commitment. At the same time, your relationship has also had the chance to become more vital, trusting and passionate and to deepen the longer you are together. Why not honor that? How much nicer it is to know each other well; to know each other's bodies intimately and to understand each other's vulnerabilities and strengths; to look and to be seen through the eyes of time, trust and compassion.

Some day we will all long for the opportunities that are in front of us in this moment. We will long for the privilege of having someone to love, to share dreams and sorrows with, support our visions, hold our hands and walk through this lifetime with. Why wait until it is too late, when the seeds of neglect have too long ago taken root, or when our precious time together here is gone? Like John Lennon's poignant song, *Life is What Happens to You While You are Busy Making Other Plans.*

I think all of us appreciate the ambiance and intimacy created by candlelight, flowers, beautiful dishes, lingering touches, meaningful conversation and specially prepared dinners. However, we tend to put these things away like good china and bring them out only for special occasions or company. I have these beautiful china teacups from England that my mother gave me. Each one is a treasure — unique, handcrafted and valuable (like each of us). We use them all of the time. My girls and I have tea parties, late night talks and special dessert evenings in which we take great pleasure in choosing our cup for the occasion. Why put them out only for company? Why not enjoy something that is special everyday? Are we not valued guests as well? Why put your relationship on hold and save special moments for Valentine's Day, birthdays or anniversaries? Instead, make a commitment to celebrate your idea of passion and connection on a regular and ongoing basis. Have it top your list of priorities and you will see dramatic changes occur.

We get so caught up in our day-to-day roles and responsibilities that we desperately need to take the opportunity to feast on each other, and feel and renew the bond that brought us together in the first place. Have your relationship magnify what you love about each other on a regular basis. Take your passion out of the cupboard, create the setting and shine.

There are many small gestures and kindnesses that only take a moment (many of which are scattered throughout this book) which are a wonderful beginning, especially when time is a factor. This chapter is about those wondrous celebrations that can help create the most intimate of occasions and deepest of shared memories. These evenings range from the more complex, to the simple, to create. Some require more daring, vulnerability and a willingness to express your desire, sexuality and attraction in a bold direct fashion; others are a loving, soft entree into more intimate waters. Of course, you can modify or play around with all of these evenings to your heart's content until they feel just right for you, kind of like Goldilocks and the Three Bears.

Whether you have the established degree of closeness you long for with your partner, or whether you are looking for ways to deepen your embrace, this chapter will spark your longing, your curiosity and your desire to be a bit more adventurous, spontaneous and playful together.

Scrub-a-dub, dub, three men in a tub (okay, maybe just one!)
an evening in the bathtub for lovers

THE THEME

Being in a bathtub with your lover is such a sensuous, romantic and relaxing experience. Something about soaking in a warm tub of bubbles softens us and makes us more vulnerable and available.

Turn this evening into a beautiful occasion. Start it with a delightful, unique invitation and then go on to exquisite room preparation, romantic music, wonderful bath products and then an array of fabulous bath-side refreshments. Learn what goes well with bubbles and bathtub games. Even aquaphobics will don their water wings just so they don't miss out on this marvelous adventure. (Rubber ducky spoken here.)

INVITATION SUGGESTIONS

Humm! To meet in the tub. How could you send out a delicious invitation. Some suggestions:

> ✉ *Attach a note to one of those little yellow rubber ducks for your partner to meet you in the tub, the time, place, etc. attached.*

> ✉ *Attach an invitation to a beautiful bar of soap. Put a label on it with all of the information, and request your partner to bring the soap with them. Or you could rewrap the soap with a written paper invitation and a funny limerick.*

127

⊠ *Send a pretty card with a packet of bath minerals in it or a washcloth with a note, I'll scrub your back, you scrub mine.*

⊠ *Deliver some Bubble bath with a humorous or romantic card you make up yourself.*

⊠ *Leave a lovely note on their pillow.*

PREPARATION

♥ *The day you are planning your bath, set up the bathroom like a sacred temple. Clean it thoroughly so it really feels like a welcoming, beautiful place. No matter how small the room, you can decorate it well.*

♥ *Get a bouquet of flowers or perhaps 1 or 2 really gorgeous ones and set them out.*

♥ *Place candles everywhere in different shapes and sizes. (Make sure they are in secure spots.) If you don't have a lot of candleholders, improvise by hollowing out apples with an apple corer and making the holes just large enough to fit a candle.*

♥ *Burn some incense or use aroma therapy to scent the room. (I suggest you burn the incense before the occasion because it can get a little overpowering while you are in such a small place. Take my word for it.)*

MUSIC

Choose your music to create the mood you want.

♪ *Go through your tapes and CDs so they are lined up and ready to go. Lots of libraries rent these out now.*

♪ *If you have a stereo system with speakers nearby, you can use that. If it is a portable player, you can leave it right outside the bathroom door. If you only have access to a radio, then turn it to a classical or jazz station, although that is always a little more unpredictable.*

♪ *Lay out two bathrobes or whatever beautiful lingerie or clothes you wish to wear when you get out. Add two large fluffy towels (it's always nice to warm them up in the dryer beforehand). Whatever the invitation said, whether it was to meet you in the tub at a certain time or meet you in the bedroom, plan accordingly. If you live with your partner and they are home and ready, fill up the tub with bubbles and invite them in.*

MORE CREATIVE FUN

Fill up a basket with fun play toys for the bath (we have a family of rubber ducks called Louie and the boys) or, those kids' windup toys are fun. You can add some fragrant soaps, bubbles to blow, loofa sponges, nail brushes, books of favorite poetry to read or a love letter that you have written.

REFRESHMENTS

A wonderful thing to do is bring food with you for a bathtub picnic. If you have a bed tray with legs on it, you can set it up and leave it by the bath. Use plastic glasses for some iced drinks. You can cut up some fruit—strawberries, melons, cherries, sections of oranges or tangerines. These are wonderful to feed to each other and you can get as elaborate as you like. I've done everything from pasta (OK that was a stretch) to chilled oysters and wine.

THE MAIN EVENT

Surprise! The bath itself! This evening can be as romantic or playful as you choose. It is a wonderful relaxing way to connect together. Share stories, feelings and thoughts. There is something about being naked together, being in warm water that softens us up. If you are in a playful mood, you can play word games like, I went on a picnic, silly games you remember, blow bubbles or paint toenails. I'll leave the details up to your imagination.

PREPARATION

Without refreshments, assuming your bathroom is clean, you only need half an hour or so. With refreshments, it depends on what you make and, if your bathroom is dirty, you be the judge!

MATERIALS

- ♥ *A bathtub and water*
- ♥ *Bubble bath or bath oils*
- ♥ *A bouquet or a few assorted flowers*
- ♥ *Candles and holders*
- ♥ *Nice fluffy towels*
- ♥ *Music you love*
- ♥ *Refreshments of choice*

YUMMY EXTRAS

- ♥ *Bath toys*
- ♥ *Massage oil*
- ♥ *Poetry books*
- ♥ *Special fragrance soaps*
- ♥ *Something special to wear when you get out of the tub*

Pleasure Palace presents...
fantasy/cabaret eve for lovers

THE THEME

Have you always wanted to put on an erotic and sexy show for your lover, but you never had the nerve or felt you lacked the know-how? Not anymore. Learn how to put together either a show, dance or act that will have them crying at your feet for more. What is the best way to invite someone?

How would you put together an act? Where do you get costumes? How do you light the room in order to create the most seductive atmosphere? Learn to set up a great stage in a one-room apartment. Would you like to be paid? What sort of refreshments would you prepare? Who will introduce your act?

By the time you read this chapter, you'll be a pro. In fact, you could probably just casually undo a few buttons and get a standing ovation!

INVITATION SUGGESTIONS

This invitation is a lot of fun. Depending upon if your partner knows you can perform (or are willing to), this evening can be a total surprise. You can reveal as much or as little as you like on the invitation so when they arrive, they might know it is for a show but that's all.

Here's how to begin.

> ☒ *Name your fantasy theatre. Let's say you name your cabaret the Pleasure Palace. All of the materials for the evening would have that name on it. You can make up a flyer for*

131

the show with the name of the cabaret, address, time, dress attire (for your guest), reservations required and the price of admission. Play with the last one. If you are planning a striptease, you could have the price of admission be $20.00 in $1.00 bills that they can appreciate you with, or you can charge them at the door.

☒ *Make up a fancy ticket for one admission to the hottest show in town. You can draw it, put it on the computer, use fancy markers or cut out some erotic pictures.*

☒ *Hand your guest a gift of a sexy piece of lingerie wrapped in an invitation to the hottest night in town, and have your lover wear it to the evening.*

☒ *Write a sexy poem.*

☒ *Deliver a bottle of champagne with the label of Pleasure Palace on it and the invitation written around that.*

☒ *Invite them to an evening of entertainment, mentioning the time, place, dress code, and nothing else, if you want the evening to be a surprise.*

NOTE:
Make sure whatever invitation you choose has an RSVP and specific time on it. It will be very important for your show preparation for the person to arrive on time.

PREPARATION

The Backstage Audition:

☒ *The first place to begin is to decide what you want to perform and then to practice it so that you feel confident and prepared. If you are planning a striptease for instance, you will want to set up a mirror in a room to practice with so you can plan all of your moves and choose the most flattering costume.*

⊠ You can rent a movie of **Gypsy Rose Lee** or some other dance movies to learn a few basic techniques. You might also have a good friend who you can practice in front of and ask for some useful feedback. A lot of us have never attempted anything like this before and might feel quite shy. I assure you that just in the act of setting it all up, putting on a costume and setting the mood, that even the simplest act will get a riproaring, foot stomping response from your partner. Why, you could probably just gaze seductively across the room and get a rave review!

⊠ If you are doing an exotic dance routine or singing, do the same thing around practicing and preparing your act. If you are reading through this but are not quite sure what you want to do, think of some skill that you have that you can turn into a tantalizing performance. Maybe it's a salsa dance, a throaty rendition of a favorite song or an enticing free form dance routine. If you still can't come up with something, ask a few close friends for ideas. Often times, we overlook our greatest strengths because they come so naturally to us.

COSTUMES

⊠ Your costume will be an important part of the success of your act. You can create a great costume from just about anything. Start off by raiding your own closet and then add bits and pieces you are missing from your friends' closets. You can use anything from a suit to strip out of, to lace outfits, gowns, high heels, lingerie combinations, scarves, belts, stockings, mini skirts or go the whole fantasy routine with something more wild and outrageous.

⊠ Men can create anything from the GQ look, to silk pants, boxers, leather outfits or any type of exotic theme costume. Goodwill, thrift and costume stores are good places to scout for buying, and for ideas.

☒ *If you don't have any lingerie that seems appropriate, go to a place like Fredericks and ask the sales clerks for some advice on putting some pieces together.*

☒ *Don't rush it. Keep playing around until you find the combination that makes you feel great.*

MUSIC

Music very much depends on personal preference and dance style. Go through your music selections and practice with different styles until you have got the combination you are happy with. If they come off of different albums, CDs or tapes, I suggest you put together a composite tape to use for your show. A few good stripping songs are, Joe Cocker's *You Can Leave Your Hat On*, Eric Clapton's *Unplugged Layla* and Sade's *Your Love is King* .

DECORATIONS

Decide where it is in your home that you are going to set up the show. If you want a cabaret atmosphere, you can set up a little table (or a few of them) just for the ambiance. Put tablecloths on them, candles and a little sign that says Reserved for _____ with your partner's name on the placecard. If you have a name for the cabaret, like the Pleasure Palace, then you can put in on a sign, with your name under it after

---

Appearing Tonight!
The Pleasure Palace presents...

You, of course!
For a limited engagement!

You can also make up a program for your guest with the Pleasure Palace name and list the routines that you will be performing.

THE STAGE

♫ *Any space you clear will do.*

♫ *For certain dance routines, you might need more room or if you are singing, you might just want a stool to sit on.*

♫ *If you want to dance on the stage and are fairly well coordinated, you can use a sturdy, large coffee table.*

♫ *A fun thing to do would be to place sparkly white Christmas lights all the way around it to give it that professional glow.*

♫ *Place candles all around the room for a soft intimate lighting effect. Enclosed lamps or votive candles work best because you can leave them unattended for a few minutes if you are behind the scenes when your guest arrives.*

Okay, so now you have your stage, your sideshow seating, your program, your entertainment marquee, you've practiced, you've got your costume on, the music is ready.

There's just one more thing.

REFRESHMENTS

Prepare what you are going to serve in advance. I would recommend keeping your refreshments really simple since your attention will be on so much else.

☛ *You can chill some wine or sodas in the refrigerator and put them out right before your guest arrives.*

☛ *You can also have a platter of finger foods or dessert out on the table.*

☛ *If the evening has the theme of Pleasure Palace, you can have the foods listed on little handmade menu signs or cards like peaches and cream or Gypsie Rose's Rose Wine.*

You get the idea.

135

THE MAIN EVENT

By showtime, everything is ready.

♥ *Get your costume on and light the candles and make sure your music is ready to go. If you want to remain hidden until your performance, or if you have made the evening a total surprise, leave instructions on the door for your guest to come in and be seated. If you decide to greet her/him at the door, put a coverup over your costume unless you want to change into it after she/he arrives.*

♥ *If you are going to collect admission, now is the time to do it. If you asked for $1.00 bills on the invitation, just tell your guest to bring them to the table and seat them. When they are comfortable, dim any lights and then excuse yourself.*

♥ *A fun idea is to tape an introduction to your performance before your music starts.*

Okay, get out there, have a ball with your performance and play it out for all it's worth! What fun to be the headline performer. What a great opportunity to be the center of your lover's attention and to give this fabulous evening as a gift.

MATERIALS

♥ *An invitation*

♥ *Practicing an act that you can perform*

♥ *A costume*

♥ *Music on tape or CD*

♥ *A table for seating your guest*

♥ *A space or table for a stage*

♥ *Cold drinks and finger foods*

♥ *Candlelight*

OPTIONAL BUT FUN

- *Twinkling Christmas lights for your stage*
- *A program, menu and Reserved sign for the table*
- *$1.00 bills to appreciate you with*
- *Posters and a program*

An  X-rated movie theatre...

THE THEME

Rent your own adult movie videos and create a great erotic and romantic setting to view them in. Transform your own home into a wonderful, sensuous and comfortable theatre. There are any number of fun ways to invite someone to participate in this unique event. Dress in something enticing for the evening. Everything you need to make the evening an exquisite, erotic success is included..

INVITATION SUGGESTIONS

Do something wonderful in this department. By now you will have caught on to this part and will want to use your creativity.

- ⊠ *Send a beautiful piece of lingerie in an envelope with an invitation for an erotic evening of movie viewing.*

- ⊠ *Write a suggestive note and send it.*

- ⊠ *Leave a sexy whispered phone invitation followed by a flower with a note attached, Can't wait for tonight.*

- ⊠ *Present a bottle of massage oil with a label invitation wrapped around it.*

- ⊠ *Buy and hand deliver a G-string, male or female, with a note wrapped around it.*

- ⊠ *Send a box of popcorn with a poem attached.*

    Note:
    On the invitation, note the time, place and suggested attire. Ask for an RSVP so that you know the show is on.

PREPARATION

You are creating a theatre in your own home.

- *Set up a beautiful environment in any part of your living space.*

- *First, clean the room thoroughly and vacuum. Place your TV and VCR where you want it to be for the night. Place candles all around the room. Make sure they are put on safe surfaces that won't easily tip over. Toss some pillows on the floor and light incense or aromatherapy. You can also lay out some towels or blankets on the floor and put out a basket containing massage oils, feathers, condoms and anything else you would enjoy.*

- *Make up a movie marquee if you would like to put it up on the wall or at the door to be seen when your guest first arrives. It could say, An Evening of Erotic Viewing for Your Pleasure, or Fantasy Pictures Presents ... and then fill in your movie titles.*

- *Make a careful selection of the movies you want to rent. Get some suggestions from friends (if they will cop to knowing any), or hopefully a helpful clerk at the movie store. Where I live, there are some wonderful sex stores that have a large selection of titles that have been reviewed and where the staff is pretty knowledgeable. They also have a catalog for mail order available under the name of Good Vibrations out of Berkeley, California (1-800-289-8423). They catalog their movies according to style, sexual preferences, content and soft and more hardcore themes.*

REFRESHMENTS

Prepare wonderful little trays of foods to share. In the invitation, you could include coupons to redeem for *the lover's platter* or *sensuous delights* and then prepare things for taste and for fun. Cut up strawberries, other types of berries and fruit. Add

fresh whipped cream, chocolate or caramel to the platter. How about oysters and cold wine or sparkling cider, or favorite finger foods to feed each other? Put all of these refreshments out on a lovely platter or tray and decorate it with a few beautiful flowers.

THE MAIN EVENT

Make sure that you put the arrival time on the invitation. Have the room set up and all of the candles lit by the arrival time. Have your refreshments laid out and the movie ready to go in the VCR. Put on whatever attire was decided for the evening—something that makes you feel desirable and sexy. Greet your lover at the door and on with the show!

MATERIALS

- ☒ *A wonderful invitation*
- ☒ *Adult movie, VCR and TV to play it*
- ☒ *Candles*
- ☒ *Blankets or towels to lay out*
- ☒ *Attire for the evening*
- ☒ *Refreshments of choice*
- ☒ *Massage oil (optional, but nice)*

A Room With A View...
photographing you

THE THEME

Here is a playful evening showing couples how to photograph each other in various erotic and romantic costumes and settings. Discover how to give yourself permission to play. Choose the most flattering attire that makes you feel your most attractive. Uncover ways to let go of stereotype images of beauty and allow your real essence, vulnerability and humor to shine through.

This chapter will leave you feeling confident, excited and with a scrapbook to cherish.

INVITATION SUGGESTIONS

You need to invite your lover to play with you, get them in the mood and attract them in.

⊠ *Send an invitation posing as a world famous photographer sent on a photo shoot to photograph the world's most beautiful man/woman. You chose them.*

⊠ *Tell your partner you have been noticing them and would love the opportunity to photograph their exquisite beauty.*

⊠ *Pretend to be a stranger writing a note that says, After seeing you, I can't get you out of my mind. Could we meet so that I could take a few photographs of you?*

⊠ *Send a note stating that you are wildly attracted to them and would give anything to be able to photograph them.*

⊠ *Send a Modeling Contract with the time and date and put in a few great pieces of lingerie to model.*

⊠ *Send a roll of film with a note saying that it needs to be completely filled with photographic images of them and send a photo album with it*

Most of us are self-conscious, feeling we are not beautiful enough or our bodies are not just right or, we compare our images to those we see in magazines. We need to let go and vanquish that point of view. Besides the fact that commercial images are unrealistic, they are also demeaning and ridiculous at best. There is nothing more desirable to a lover than the gift of their beloved allowing their beauty, vulnerability and love to shine through. This is a wonderful gift to treasure and you will appreciate having a record of your love as the years pass.

PREPARATION

THE CAMERA:

♥ *Start off by making sure that you have a good camera to use. For regular film, there are labs that will develop more risqué photos for you. Find out what their policy on nudity is, and how discreet they are, as well as their reputation. If you don't want to deal with that or, you live in a place where access to a lab is not so easily obtained, use an instant Polaroid camera instead.*

♥ *Start by giving yourself a few options of background, scenery and costumes. You can use your bedroom for one scenario, a living room, set up some funny ideas for the kitchen or even use your bathtub. Pull out any beautiful sheets, blankets or accessories that you think would be fun.*

♥ *Try photographing the empty space first and experiment with the lighting with a roll of film. When the actual evening happens, you will be much more prepared and get better results.*

COSTUMES

Get out all of the different clothing and outfits that you love. Take out silk underwear, stockings, high heels, silk boxers, favorite jeans or evening attire. You can also buy a special delicious gift for your partner as a surprise.

An important element here is that the person being photographed feels great in the clothing to choose from. You can also put on some favorite music and have them free float around dancing and get some great pictures that way.

REFRESHMENTS

Make it into a party!

- *Serve whatever drinks and food you like.*
- *Use foods that are sensuous and fun to photograph—whipped cream, strawberries, pies, or whatever you like.*

I saw some great pictures a woman had done where she had covered her breasts entirely with whipped cream and was eating strawberries. The photographs were playful and delightful.

THE MAIN EVENT

When your lover arrives, have your place decorated with a lot of different settings where he or she can be photographed.

- *Set up a little wardrobe area with changes of clothing, a mirror and brush.*
- *Set up flattering lighting that works with your camera.*
- *Turn on some music and have fun!*
- *You can also take turns photographing each other.*

145

- *Buy a photo album for the occasion and you will have yourself a treasure forever, to say nothing of the fun you will have creating it.*

MATERIALS

- *A great invitation*
- *A camera and film*
- *Various costumes to wear*
- *A few decorated settings for photographing*
- *Refreshments*
- *Music*
- *A photo album*

Section

Five

Got
Joy?

Five-Minute Gestures of Delight

This is the place to look in the book if you would love to do something wonderful but have only a small window of time at the moment. You know those days—your dog throws up on the way out the door, the sink is full of dishes, the car is in the shop, your computer is down and you are on deadline. Your life is just a full affair. So here are some quick ways to express yourself. Start in the home and move out into the world.

This is one of my favorite acts of kindness to share...

> It was around holiday time and I was at the grocery store. Everyone had their carts full of various holiday foods. Usually I am pretty friendly to everyone around me but on this particular day, I was feeling quite moody and glum. So I pretty much kept to myself.
>
> As I was gathering up my groceries after having paid for them, I noticed the man behind me. All he had were two bouquets of flowers in his cart. I remember thinking that was quite odd since he didn't even have one item of food, just flowers. I glanced at the flowers and then at him and in spite of my mood, I enjoyed the idea of someone receiving those flowers.
>
> As I started to head out the door, he handed me one of the bouquets, 'Here, these are for you.' He couldn't have realized the power those flowers held for me. The kindness of that gesture broke through my moodiness

and opened my heart in such gratitude. What a delight to be the recipient of such a thoughtful and surprising gesture. You really have no idea the rippling effects that your kindnesses have for others. In one moment, something you do can be passed on a hundred times in that one day.

♡ BETH C.

DELIGHTING PARTNERS, SPOUSES OR LOVERS

♥ *Leave love and appreciation notes stuck to the mirrors around the bathroom.*

♥ *Leave a card on the seat of the car.*

♥ *Put a wonderful note in a briefcase or a handbag or lunch box.*

♥ *Put a little heart on a key ring with a note attached as the key to my heart.*

♥ *Pack a picnic lunch and surprise each other. Tuck an invitation into a purse or briefcase.*

♥ *Send an invitation for a beautiful dinner even if you get out to dinner a lot. Make the gesture of an invitation. It shows your appreciation and that you don't take each other for granted.*

♥ *Leave soft, loving messages on the phone machine, or sing them when you feel brave.*

♥ *Meet each other at the door and express your love for one another. Express it first before tumbling out the day's frustrations. It will change the mood immediately. Greet each other with praise instead of complaint.*

♥ *Keep a wishing jar at home for all of your fantasies and wishes. Each of you choose a different color of paper to write them down on, and then plan an evening to start pulling the papers out and fulfilling them.*

♥ *Have a bubble bath prepared for your partner when they walk in the door. Lead them upstairs (or down the hall) and put some soft music on. Light a candle.*

♥ *Prepare a special lunch and put a loving note inside of it. Tell them you can't wait until the end of the day when you can see them.*

♥ *Bring their morning tea or coffee to the bedroom. Serve it on a tray with a love note.*

♥ *Warm a towel for a bath or shower in the dryer. Be waiting to wrap them up, hug them, and tell them how you love them; then you can disappear (if you want to).*

♥ *When you leave a message about groceries, kids or errands, start it out with how much you love and appreciate sharing your lives together.*

♥ *Leave each other with a real sense of praise, gratitude and love when you part each day.*

♥ *Put a little card on their windshield wiper. Have it say, Drive safely, you're precious. You can be sure they will approach the road very differently that day.*

♥ *Get in the car and find a quiet place to drive. Open the windows, light a candle and sit back and watch the stars. Let go of the stresses of the day. Dream out loud. (Okay, good for much longer than five minutes.)*

♥ *Play a favorite song and leave it on someone's answering machine. (Hopefully, it's a local call.)*

♥ *If you are going to a movie or play and you have the music to it, call up and leave a message with the song in the background and just say Really looking forward to seeing you tonight.*

♥ *Write out a card and leave it somewhere special to be found, in a pocket of a jacket, or underneath your pillow.*

♥ *Show up with a balloon for no apparent reason.*

♥ *Wrap yourself up as a gift with a bow around you. Who wouldn't love to unwrap that?*

You get the idea.

Minutes of Delight with Your Children

This is a place where the effects of your praise are so blatantly obvious. Anything you do creates such instant recognition and joy with children. Even a teenager who will act out or hold their feelings in, will start to soften with praise.

- *Leave notes around the house--sticky notes with anything they have done that you appreciate, even if it's teeny, tiny, small.*
    - ✉ *I appreciate that you put your stuff away when you made a snack,*
    - ✉ *Thanks for washing out the tub when you had a shower,*
    - ✉ *You look particularly beautiful today,*
    - ✉ *Boy, you work hard in sports. I admire your determination. I love the way you are always willing to put yourself out there,*
    - ✉ *You have a lot of courage,*
    - ✉ *You really seem to understand math well, maybe you could help explain it to me or help me with my bills.*

- *Leave little treats around. Some favorite things that say Just because I love you, or I really value you. Put a little note on it that says, The elf dropped by just for fun.*

- *Make their bed as a surprise. Leave a little note that says Courtesy of one little elf found wandering past your room.*

> *One day, I walked in my room and there was an angel pin on my bed from a little elf and my bed was made and perfectly straightened out. On my night table was my name written with flowers and grass and twigs and it said 'Courtesy of a little elf.'*

152

🕊 *Make a treasure hunt of clues to the dinner table. It totally delights children. Leave a note with a snack after school with a little elf print on it saying just cause I love you, thought you would enjoy this.*

🕊 *Create moods together. Plan a bubble bath. Put on some lovely music. Invite your children a little differently into your lives.*

🕊 *Before bed, spend five minutes cuddling up, sharing dreams, wishes or a favorite childhood memory. Kids love to hear stories about you as a child.*

YOUNGER KIDS
(MIGHT TAKE A FEW MINUTES LONGER)

★ *Make up a little game with tickets. They each get a ticket or an angel card for doing something right. You are always looking to catch them doing something right. They can trade their little cards in for privileges or you can open up a little store where they can buy things with their cards—tiny little things that they usually enjoy and that you might have around the house anyway.*

★ *Play a game of beat the clock for getting ready for bed. Be the MC and watch how quickly they move. Become the MC at kitchen time or cleanup and keep encouraging them as they go along. Set the timer for tasks you know they can accomplish. (Say, three minutes for teeth brushing.) Give them a coupon to redeem if they Beat the Clock.*

★ *Make a game of cleaning up by colors or by numbers. For instance, "Pick up two red things and then come back to me," or "Pick up three small things and then come back to me." You would be amazed at how quickly children move when they are having fun with something. Kind of like us.*

FIVE MINUTES TO DELIGHT
PARENTS, RELATIVES AND THOSE FAR AWAY

Find ways that you can honor people and make occasions special. Let people know what they mean to you while you have an opportunity to tell them in life.

✉ *Write notes or letters. On my birthday one year, I wrote a letter to my parents thanking them for everything they have done for me; for all of the birthday parties, the outings, the carpooling, the trips to the dentist, the help with homework, the talks, nursing me through illness, that sort of thing.*

✉ *Pay attention to the things that they might enjoy that are no cost; newspaper articles, clippings, inspirational quotes you find, photographs of your family. Send them off. People really appreciate them.*

FIVE MINUTES OF DELIGHT
OUT INTO THE WORLD

🌑 *Take five extra minutes and be gentle in your car. There is nothing to be gained by aggressive, impatient behavior. Relax, listen to music and wave someone else through.*

🌑 *Pay someone's fare at the toll booth. Ask the attendant to ask that person to spread one delightful gesture themselves.*

🌑 *Give out wrapped chocolates or treats to people that take care of you or whose services help you out in the course of the day--whether it is the person who changes the oil in your car, or a bagger at the checkout stand.*

🌑 *When I get change sometimes, I drop the shiniest coins on the pavement. Let someone pick it up for their lucky day.*

154

☯ *Offer someone in distress a meal, a warm pair of gloves, or whatever you can in the moment. We are all responsible for, and connected to, each other.*

☯ *Invite your co-workers to a picnic, with each one bringing something. If the weather is nice, go outside. If it's not, spread a blanket on the floor at work or on a table. Make a little card for each person in the group and write down something you really enjoy about them.*

☯ *Start thanking people for the services they provide for you. If you belong to a gym and you see someone mopping up the wet floor, stop and thank them for the job — I appreciate the job that you do and that you make it safe for me to walk here. Thank you.*

☯ *Say grace or a prayer of gratitude for the gifts you have been given in your lives. Bless others as well.*

☯ *Thank people for the work they do that makes life much easier and nicer for your family.*

☯ *When you go to the grocery store and you see the butcher or the fish person or the person who chooses the produce, thank them for the time that they take to prepare and to do such a nice job. See it as an offering from these people and treat it as such. Most people don't take the time to let someone know how they feel. Wouldn't it be lovely if we felt there was real regard out there for what we do? Thank the trash people who handle the garbage and the ones who come and recycle and the ones who clean the street. Where would we be without all of their help? Spread delight and joy. Let them know that their lives and their work make a difference to you.*

☯ *If you see someone looking lost or needing help, offer it without being asked. Offer directions, open and close doors, or carry a heavy bag for someone.*

155

☥ *Slow down when you see it is difficult for someone crossing the street. They have enough of a challenge without our added impatience.*

☥ *Pick up litter you see. If everyone would pick up one can or piece of trash each day, think how beautiful our streets and cities would look.*

☥ *Shop at independent stores that offer great service and that support your community or schools. Pay a little more if you need to and buy less so we can all thrive and stay in business.*

☥ *Write or call your elected officials on issues you feel strongly about and that impact your lives or the lives of your children. Stand up for what you believe in.*

☥ *Commit to praising others more often. Everything grows in an atmosphere of love and kindness.*

☥ *If you are a manager or boss to others, let people know you appreciate their talent and effort. Remember we are all human. When you see signs of fatigue or stress or unhappiness, give them a safe space or a few hours off to relax. You will be amazed at the loyalty and effort you receive back.*

☥ *Smile more. It's contagious.*

☥ *Laugh more. Laughter is a great healer.*

☥ *Acknowledge more. Do you have people whose services make your life easier? A great car mechanic? A reliable plumber? A shoe repair person? Tailor? Dry Cleaner? Gardener? Write a brief note letting them know how you appreciate them. Drop it off on your next visit.*

☥ *Forgive. If we all spent five minutes a day in forgiveness of ourselves and others, we could transform everything. It is probably the most powerful and loving gesture you can make on the planet.*

♪ ♪ ♪ ♪ ♪ ♪ ♪ ♪ ♪ ♪ ♪ ♪ ♪ ♪

Maestro,
pass the baton
please!

creating your own events

As you read this book, I hope the idea has been planted as to how to invite people, plan and celebrate occasions. Now, how about planning your own unique celebrations? I am going to share some ideas with you about how to create the process for yourself so that you can come up with your own memorable events to celebrate your lives together. (Don't forget to celebrate your own achievements as well, which I hope you acknowledge liberally.)

> One time a special friend of mine made plans to go on a fishing expedition on a boat called the S.S. Salty Lady. Due to work conflicts and demands, he had to cancel the trip. Because I knew he was terribly disappointed, I decided to create the entire adventure in the bedroom. I mounted glow-in-the-dark stars on the ceiling and borrowed a CD of ocean sounds. I turned the bed into a boat with lots of cushions and packed a cooler of chips, beer, and snacks.
>
> I put blue tissue on the floor and cut out paper waves to place on the water for authenticity. I attached magnets to cardboard fish that I had bought at the party store and placed them on the "ocean floor." I made fishing poles out of long sticks with string and used paper clips for hooks. Bait was a tin of candy gummy worms. I made a life preserver that said "S.S. Salty Lady" cut out of posterboard and attached it to the bed post. We sat on the bed with our fishing poles, listening to the music under the stars, ate snacks and had a truly magical evening.

157

Beginning to Create

The Blank Canvas:

To begin to create, the first thing I suggest is to give yourself a huge canvas in your mind about what you want to celebrate. Picture all kinds of possible scenarios with no limitations of any sort imposed. Close your eyes and get the feel of it.

Some Helpful Thoughts to Consider:

Ask yourself—What mood is it that I want to share? How do I feel being there? How do the guests feel? Is it a family occasion? Are kids invited? Who is included in this celebration? What is it that I want to celebrate? Is it an individual achievement, the bond of friendship, a new collaboration, a marriage, the birth of a new life? Maybe it's a romantic celebration. Perhaps it's a wonderful surprise for a child?

Ideas for Creating:

Once you have even a vague idea of what you want to celebrate, start thinking of the person or persons you are creating this for—what would they enjoy? What do they relish? Use a large pad and a set of markers to write down your ideas. In random order, write down every possible idea. If you still haven't conceived of a theme or activity, you can easily overcome this creative block. With the person in mind, just start writing a complete list of anything and everyone they appreciate or enjoy. For instance, they love: poetry, the color red, artwork, tulips, oatmeal cookies, surprises, breakfast in bed, lasagna, rainbows, their dream vacation is Italy, the opera, formal attire...

You get the idea.

Begin combining things — the total concept will emerge naturally and spontaneously with each idea or step leading to the next. Initially, disregard obvious barriers such as cost, feasibility and practicality. Without these restrictive considerations, you will have complete freedom to be creative, innovative and uncensored.

Once the idea and details have been formed, it is surprisingly easy to reduce or eliminate expenses or leap over perceived obstacles. It is fun and possible to create the ambience of an authentic café in your own home without the expense and inconvenience of traveling to Italy or going for pastries in a Parisian café.

THE CREATION:

Let's say that the occasion is a milestone birthday and the celebration will be an evening at home, a deux. Referring to the inventory list for inspiration, since they love surprises, you know it must be a mysterious, magical date encompassing their favorite things. Because they are fond of poetry, you may feature that on the invitation. You can copy a treasured poem or write your own love poem (Roses are red ... will be just fine).

Reviewing the list, let's consider different possibilities.

❧ *One idea is to create an Evening in Italy which includes their dream vacation, their favorite food, their love of flowers, formal wear and the color red. You can choose a red checkered tablecloth, a vase of fresh flowers and, depending on your budget, flowers strewn throughout the home, including fresh, fragrant petals on the floor leading to the bedroom. Specify the time, date, location and appropriate attire without mentioning the details of your plan.*

159

❧ At the library, select beautiful art books featuring Italy and Italian painters. Some libraries lend CDs or you can buy opera music to play softly in the background and for dancing after dinner. You can prepare a pasta dish, lasagna, or any of their favorite entrees, served with a salad, bread and wine (or perhaps a non-alcoholic beverage). As a surprise, after dinner, you could go to a local coffee house for espressos and biscotti.

CREATE FURTHER AND DEEPER:

❧ Using your imagination, create characters to play. Or you can rent an Italian movie with English subtitles. If it's in the budget, buy tickets to the opera. If not, rent a video of a favorite opera or choose a CD from one of their favorite operas. Mount posters from travel agencies on the wall. A nice detail would be to have a loaded camera on hand to capture this special occasion on film for a permanent keepsake.

ANOTHER POSSIBLE SCENARIO:

❧ Start the day with a surprise breakfast in bed and place a single fresh flower on the tray. While they are eating, recite some of their favorite poetry between bites of waffle. (A nice romantic touch, don't you think?) Put on your finery and leisurely tour a local art museum. On the way home, visit a cozy café for a cappuccino and cookies.

RITUAL OR RITE OF PASSAGE

If you are celebrating a ritual or a passage, ask probing questions. Is this a passage that has both losses to grieve and new opportunities to anticipate? Is someone letting go of something to make space for something else? If so, you can view the celebration from both sides. To create the occasion, ask yourself what is being released? For instance, is it caretaking? Is it a role that is now obsolete; perhaps the childbearing years, and if so, then what will fill the void? In this case, you are moving into a phase of expanded freedom, time and creativity. If you are leaving a job that no longer suits you, you are letting go of routine, familiarity and comfort; but you are also inviting in learning, excitement and challenge.

> *I wanted to have a tubal ligation. I was certain that I did not want any other children and I was tired of not-always predictable birth control. Having been supremely healthy my entire life, it was hard to imagine subjecting myself to voluntary general anesthesia and surgery. I was certain of my decision but I was scared. I gathered some friends together and asked a friend of mine who was a massage therapist and healer, if she would conduct the celebration. There were 4 of us in the room. She had cleansed the whole room and it smelled wonderful and there was soft music playing in the background. I lay on the massage table and did some deep breathing to relax. I did a meditation of my own, just tuning into my concerns. We then blessed and thanked my body for its health, strength and for the two children that it had birthed. With the help of friends, we said goodbye to that time in life and welcomed in a new time of creative fertility and birth. We sang together, said prayers and I had a massage. When I got up from the table, it felt like the fear had just walked out the door. We sat and celebrated, had wonderful snacks together and I left. I was still concerned but I had great peace about it.*

> *The next day, the surgery went like a breeze. I felt totally prepared because I had let go of what I needed to. I had no unfinished business and was ready to embrace something new. I left the hospital without taking an aspirin. What a great way to welcome in a new phase of my life.*

> ℘*Susan R.*

A Brand New Relationship or Friend

If you are not sure of someone's preferences because it's a newer relationship, ask questions. What are your favorite childhood memories? What brings you great joy? What would you love to do more of if you had the time? What are your favorite foods? It's really a matter of beginning to pay attention to what it is that people tell you. What haven't they done for a long time that they used to enjoy? Then take all of that information and use it. Scramble it up and see what you can create. I know you're imaginative, talented and brilliant!

> *I have a friend who loves bubble baths, oysters, Anchor Steam beer (available in San Francisco), candlelight — Get the picture?*

Okay, so you've never had a birthday party in the tub with oysters and beer but, it's not too late. It's a matter of using your intuition and developing it in ways that you might not have given yourself permission to in the past. It also does not have to be elaborate, expensive or time-consuming. What do you want to communicate? What do you feel? Find a fun, innovative way to convey your emotions and gratitude.

BIG HINT – KEEP A SECRET SLEUTH FILE

It helps to keep a little notebook to jot down ideas. For instance, the next time someone casually remarks "My favorite movie of all time is ...," or "Don't you just love daffodils, they make even the grayest day happy" ... Make a note of it. Then the next time you want to do something fun, buy a small bouquet of daffodils; rent their all time favorite movie (which you know because you have written it down in your trusty little book) and show up, occasion or date in hand!

Reclaiming the Treasure...
remaking holiday celebrations

CHRISTMAS

This book is not the place to address the religious significance of this holiday, or any other holiday for that matter. Each one of us has our own personal beliefs, traditions and spiritual practices that enrich our lives and deepen our faith. What we can look at though, is how we can begin to make different choices that reflect our generosity, our love and our intentions with our loved ones and out in the world.

Most of our holidays are dripping with consumerism that makes us feel overwhelmed, overspent and undernourished. We can't keep up with the demands that are placed on us. If you took a survey and asked people you know how many of them want to end the spending frenzy and change their approach to the holidays, it would likely be at least 8 out of 10. We are all hooked in, unable to find a gracious way out, because each one of us wants to express our giving nature. Even if we have attempted to shorten our gift list or obligations, when someone gives us a gift or extends an invitation, it feels awkward and uncomfortable not to reciprocate. The stakes then keep escalating and we end up feeling financially and spiritually bankrupt, as well as emotionally and physically exhausted.

So here are some ideas to help shift the focus of the holidays away from frenzy and more toward intimacy and relaxation—to have gift giving be less from the marketplace and more of a heart-felt expression.

FIRST SUGGESTION

A good beginning is to decide to eliminate or replace what doesn't feel good about the way you currently celebrate the holiday. Make your *To Buy* gift list shorter. Ask yourself what you truly want to give to people. How would you like to express your love? Your compassion? You might decide to have the holiday season be focused around your intimates; and then if you wish, take your generosity out into the world. To really consider the gifts you offer or the celebrations you want to create, ask yourself the following questions:

1. *What do I choose to express this holiday season?*

2. *What is it that we want to create either individually, as a couple, family, or group of friends?*

3. *What activities do we enjoy doing together?*

4. *What do I want most out of this holiday time? Is it intimacy? More shared time together? To give something back to the community? More time with family and friends? More time for reflection?*

If you look at your motivations first, and what you would really like, you can easily begin to redesign your holidays to reflect that.

WONDERFUL LOW-COST GIFT IDEAS

★ *Give the gift of an uninterrupted evening of sharing what you love about each other.*

★ *Spend an evening taking out photographs of family and friends and make small gift albums of your times together. Include fondest memories.*

★ Spend an evening with close friends going around the room praising and sharing what you really appreciate and love about your friendship and each other.

★ Spend the day making cookies, gingerbread houses or treats to bring to friends, shelters, nursing homes or hospitals.

★ Clean out all of your unused belongings and make a gift donation to a local shelter.

★ Spend the evening writing letters to important people in your life, telling them how you feel about them and sharing some of your fondest memories over the last year.

★ Make things together as a family. Look through this book (and others) for gift ideas and spend the afternoon or evenings making simple gifts that everybody can participate in, regardless of the age or skill level. Delegate a way for each person to participate. Have someone write the card, someone label, wrap, stir dough, package, put music on and clean up.

★ Get a gathering of friends together and choose a simple meal to share. Instead of exchanging gifts with each other, make something or bring canned goods to the gathering and donate them at the end of the evening to your local food bank.

★ Get a group together and designate a favorite charity or cause and support that, instead of individual gifts to each other.

★ Spend an afternoon together baking and exchanging holiday cookies and treats. Have everyone bring beautiful tins and boxes to share so you can leave with pre-packaged gifts.

★ Plan an outdoor hike to appreciate nature, the woods, the ocean. Spend more time in contemplation and gratitude.

★ Make a scrapbook together. Buy a few big scrapbooks and glue sticks and keep them as an ongoing family project.

★ Ask your friends to do a kind and generous gesture, *thinking* of you instead of shopping for you. What a way to celebrate friendship.

★ Suggest that your office do something together that inspires positive feelings for each other. Instead of an office party, sit down and share your dreams or the important things in your life. Put an end to negative gossip. Plan a Christmas meal and ask everyone to bring something in and talk about one thing that they are grateful for at work. (This will be a big stretch for a lot of folks.)

★ Have everybody bring in donations of canned goods and clothing and support one deserving family during the holidays instead of buying gifts for each other at the office. Create a celebration for a family who ordinarily wouldn't be able to have one.

★ Arrange an evening for singing your favorite holiday songs together. Copy songbooks for each other. If you feel shy, sing along to some favorite tapes. Serve refreshments.

★ Plan an evening with friends to share your favorite holiday memories and stories. Have everyone bring a snack.

★ Invite close friends over. Make popcorn and watch feel-good movies together.

With Children

★ Invite your family to put on pj's or sweat pants, make some hot chocolate, put it in a thermos, put on a holiday music tape, and drive around enjoying the beautiful Christmas lights.

★ Support a deserving family as a holiday project. Decide on a budget together and have the children chip in with some of their

166

own money. Let them shop for the gifts, wrap them up and deliver them. It will make them feel good. Have children clean their old or unused toys out, wrap them, and donate them to a hospital or shelter.

★ *String cranberries, popcorn and some other old fashioned decorations for a tree.*

★ *Watch wonderful classic movies together.*

★ *Bake cookies for yourselves and bake extras to give out to nursing homes, hospitals or shelters.*

★ *Build a snowman (if you live in snow), have a snowball fight, come in and have hot chocolate.*

★ *Cuddle up in front of the fire. Tell stories about your childhood.*

★ *Bring out old photographs to look at and games to play. Spend the evening enjoying the albums and playing games together.*

★ *Invite them to a pajama party. Have a good old fashioned pillow fight.*

★ *Listen to favorite beautiful music together.*

★ *Read inspiring stories together of the real heroes in life; people who triumph over remarkable obstacles. Praise real courage.*

★ *Start a new tradition Pass on a Treasure. Find something that you have, that your child loves, and when you are ready, pass it on as a treasured gift. You can do this every year. You can even make a special box to put it in, and use the same box every year to pass your treasured gift on.*

★ *Send an invitation to your child, and their favorite stuffed animal or doll, to a holiday tea party. Create a festive occasion. Dress up in special outfits, light candles or just turn on the twinkling lights. Create a beautiful area. Serve a favorite dessert or Christmas cookies with a favorite beverage. Create a little menu* as a souvenir. You can even name your tea house. If your child doesn't read yet, put pictures beside the items that they can order. Maybe a parent, a friend or a sibling would like to play "server." This will be easily as enjoyable as a special restaurant occasion, and you don't have to spend a lot of money, fight traffic, parking or crowds.

VALENTINE'S DAY

Throughout this book, there are ideas that translate well as Valentine's gifts and celebrations, so you might want to browse through the gift and adventure sections for some ideas.

For those of you in intimate relationships, every idea in the *Stoking The Flames* section would be a fabulous surprise and make your partner jump for joy. And, here are a few more ideas to pull out of the romance hat that require just a little time and nary a farthing.

- ♥ *Create a basket of bulbs and seeds for favorite flowers as a reminder of your growing and sustaining love (instead of mega-priced roses).*

- ♥ *Make homemade favorite treats, beautifully wrapped (instead of a box of chocolates).*

- ♥ *Plan a special romantic picnic spread outside (weather permitting, if you live in the tropics) or inside, with candlelight (instead of a very crowded, over-priced restaurant).*

- ♥ *Make an expressive handmade card or poster.*

- ♥ *Create coupons for all kinds of nurturing gestures and kindnesses, (i.e., good for a massage, a foot rub, breakfast in bed, a least favorite errand, a home-cooked meal), hand-drawn or created on the computer.*

- ♥ *Put together a music tape of favorite love songs.*

♥ *Create a heart treasure hunt. Cut out clues in the shape of hearts (or buy stickers). Have the clues lead you to a treasure chest. Inside the treasure chest, have notes written about everything you love about that person.*

♥ *Offer a gift of uninterrupted time on a weekly basis. This may seem simplistic, but with our busy lives, it's not. Make a certificate to commit to a certain time in the week that is just about your intimacy or private time together.*

♥ *Frame a favorite photograph of the two of you and enclose a beautiful sentiment.*

♥ *Create a homemade booklet, entitled "101 Ways I Love You" (or 50, or whatever you've written) with their picture on the cover. Write something you love about your partner on every page.*

If you are not presently in an intimate relationship, or if you are experiencing estrangement in your current relationship, this holiday can dawn with nervous trepidation. Or maybe a relationship has recently ended through separation or death. Regardless of your circumstances, there are so many different kinds of love you have in your life for which you can express gratitude on Valentines Day. You can celebrate love of friends, parents, children, colleagues and other kindred spirits.

FOR KIDS

♥ *Create a heart treasure hunt with clues that lead you to a treat. For younger kids, buy heart-shaped stickers, stick them to the floor or carpet, and have them follow the stickers somewhere to a special treat.*

♥ *Serve heart-shaped food for the day. Some suggestions would be waffles, pancakes, sandwiches (use a cookie cutter), homemade pizzas and pasta in the shape of hearts.*

♥ *Serve foods in red and pink. Some suggestions would be strawberry milkshakes, smoothies, pink ice cream, tomato soup, minestrone soup, radishes, red peppers and tomatoes cut up, pasta, and toast cut out with a cookie cutter topped with jam.*

♥ *Create love coupons for privileges on cards with hearts on them. Have them be redeemable for an extra bedtime story, a favorite snack, a trip to the park....*

BIRTHDAY CELEBRATIONS

I have a tradition in my women's group that I would like to pass on. We started this a few year's ago. When our birthdays come, we ask the birthday person what they would like to have supported at this time or what feels meaningful in their life. Would they like a new job? A relationship? A better situation with the kids?

The idea is to honor who that person is. For example, for one birthday, we celebrated the mother/lover/wise woman in one of our friends. Each of us took one of the roles that she played in life and wrote down all of the wonderful strengths and ways we saw her excel in that area.

Then we dressed up for that part (for instance, one of us dressed as earth mother and did a little performance about that part of her). It gave her an opportunity to see herself and to really feel her strengths. Then we presented her with what we had written as her birthday gift.

♥ *SUSAN Z.*

FUN ADULT BIRTHDAY IDEAS

♪ *Acknowledge people in as many ways as you can think of. Write out a list of their wonderful qualities and set it out on the table, mail it to them, or wrap it up as a gift.*

♫ *Support a dream. If someone you know has a dream or something they really want to accomplish, create a little ceremony affirming it for them. Help them come up with a plan to accomplish their goal. Have your gift be to coach, inspire and cheer them on.*

♫ *Write a story, "It's a Wonderful Life." Let them know how important their presence is in your life and in the world. Think of all of the ways that they have made a difference in your life and let them know.*

♫ *Do something fun with your gift! Make them a treasure hunt to find their present.*

CREATE A MAGICAL *JUST FOR YOU* DAY

Forget the one present, cake and limp rendition of Happy Birthday. How about having the kind of day you haven't had since you were a kid (if ever!).

Think of things that the birthday person would really love and then fill the day up with surprises. Here are a few suggestions:

🕊 *Drop them off at a favorite breakfast place (and have the bill already handled), or serve them a favorite breakfast at home.*

🕊 *Take them to their favorite hiking, biking or walking place.*

🕊 *Rent a movie that they love and pop popcorn.*

🕊 *Arrange lunch or coffee with some of their best friends.*

🕊 *Take them shopping (only if they like it—for some it's torture) to choose a birthday treat.*

🕊 *Arrange a swimming time, a workout, a steam or hot tub. Drop them off at a gym and pick them up when they are ready.*

🕊 *Present them with a stack of favorite magazines, soft music and uninterrupted time to read.*

🕊 *Make dinner reservations at a favorite place or create one of our adventures in this book.*

❦ *Make a favorite meal.*

❦ *Put on a skit or do a funny family performance (if that kind of talent runs in your family).*

❦ *Play DJ and spin their favorite songs for an hour.*

CELEBRATING KIDS' BIRTHDAYS

I got a note on my birthday saying we were going on a surprise adventure. I didn't know where I was going. On the morning we left, my mother's friend showed up at the door with a hat and tie on and said he was our limousine service. He took us to the train station. It turns out we were going to take the train to Old Sacramento. We went on a horse and carriage ride and I got birthday money to spend in the stores. When we came back, our limousine driver was waiting for us holding up a pad that had our names and our destination home written on it. I tipped the driver a dollar. It was so much fun.

♈ *JESSIE S.*

★ *Put little notes around the house about your child's great qualities.*

★ *Plan a surprise adventure. Even if you are going to the park to play, you can make it special by hiding little clues. Then they find something like a pail and a shovel to play with.*

★ *Make a special occasion for you and your child or your family. Don't rush around with party invitations for 20 kids. Spend the day doing kids' things together that you don't usually have time for.*

★ *Walk through the woods, go to the beach, search for shells, build a castle together.*

★ *Take out all of the messy art projects that are usually postponed and make things together.*

★ Snuggle up and read a pile of favorite books.

★ Bake something unusual and wonderful. Have your birthday child cook a favorite birthday dinner with you.

★ Take your child to a party store and get them a paper chef's hat or crown to wear for the birthday meal preparation. Let them be in charge of the menu.

★ Tell them the story of their birth. Let them know how special and unique they are and how meaningful and wonderful it is to have them in your lives. Take out pictures of them and show them how they have grown over the years.

★ Set up a little birthday wishing well. Have a beautiful bowl or special container to use. Collect pretty colored rocks or favorite stones. Sit with your child and light some candles and put the wishing well in a special place. Fill the bowl with water. Tell them as they place each stone in the water to affirm and wish for what they would like in this new year.

★ They can have as many wishes as they like. Then other family members can choose a rock and wish something for them.

WITH OLDER CHILDREN

✦ Have your older children release things they want to let go of this year at the *Wishing Well*. Before they make their new wishes, write down the things they would like to eliminate, such as fighting with my sister, or biting my nails... Then burn the paper (over the sink) and let those things go symbolically. Then begin the wishing process.

      ❦   *Make a huge banner out of paper or poster board and put it up in the room and write everything on there that you love about them. Have friends and family members contribute. Hang it up on the day of their birthday so it is the first thing that they see in the morning. You can bet they'll hold onto that for a long time to come.*

CREATING YOUR OWN MEANINGFUL HOLIDAYS

We love to celebrate the start of the Jewish New Year. We like to go up to the mountains at sunrise and write out our wishes for the coming year and have a picnic. This year we couldn't make it until late afternoon and it was getting pretty cold. We packed a picnic and went up to the mountain and set it out in the picnic area. We started to get cold so we got into the car. We lit votive candles, rolled down the windows, popped some beautiful soft music in the cassette player, and laid the seats all the way back. We all held hands and watched the sky darken and the stars come out and made our wishes that day. It was an impromptu and memorable celebration.

                          ✱ *JAMIE S.*

CELEBRATE INDIVIDUAL ACHIEVEMENT

Has someone you know achieved a significant goal or passed a difficult milestone? Returned to school? Made the team? Taken on a new challenge? Finished a major project? Worked really hard on something? Mastered a new skill? Why not acknowledge it in a fun way? Create a special evening for them. For instance, has someone you know published something recently? Make a Famous Author Comes to Town headline and paste it on a newspaper. Have a writer's evening.

CELEBRATE COURAGE

Many of the things that we are required to do take so much courage; trying out for a school play or community theatre, taking on a big project or a new position, the first job back in the work world after raising children, or a new tentative step somewhere. All of these efforts can be recognized and rewarded. Create a celebration for that person. Make them a certificate of courage. Find a way to help inspire them through the most difficult moments. Let them know that you are cheering them on.

DAYS OF GRATITUDE

Spend a day focusing on positive things in your life.

- *What is it that really works for you and that you would like more of?*

- *What is it that you really appreciate?*

- *Who is it that you really love and that loves you in return? Let people know.*

- *Spend time writing letters.*

- *Have gratitude for your health, appreciate your body, appreciate your surroundings, including the clothes in your closet, the food in your refrigerator, the books on your shelf, the photographs in your albums, the memories that you share. So much of the time, we spend focusing on lack or what we feel is missing in our lives. Instead spend the day deepening your sense of appreciation for all the things that are working wonderfully in your life.*

CELEBRATE PLAY

- *Take out crayons, markers, paper, glitter, wood, glue, model airplanes, clay, whatever it is that you love.*

175

❧ *Spend the day just having fun creating. Is there a project you'd love to tackle, or a special craft that you have always wanted to have time to do. Maybe it's something that you want to sew, paint, build, or something special that you might like to cook. You might want to bake an elaborate cake that you have never had the time to do.*

❧ *Spend the day playing.*

❧ *Put music on, take your materials out, put on a smock or sloppy clothes and have a ball.*

CELEBRATING YOUR OLDER CHILDREN

❧ *Provide an evening of unconditional understanding to your adolescent. Send an invitation that says, "I will be here to listen to every complaint, dissatisfaction and fear without comment or judgment. I will provide a listening ear and a great snack." Turn off the phone, clear the evening and just hang out. You will learn a lot.*

❧ *Call it a celebration of honoring who they are. Make a special cake or dessert. Keep all conversation positive. What do you love about them? What have they accomplished that is particularly meaningful to them? What do you see about the courage they have in life, goals they have gone after and things they have achieved. Let them know. Have their siblings join it. Praise can become contagious. The pre-teen and teen years are a time of turmoil, when relationships can be strained and become more distant. Even though your child might not be able to acknowledge it now, this will be a powerful and wonderful gift for them. It is a time they especially need to hear how special they are and a time when they have the most difficulty asking for anything.*

Ode to Cyrano

*love letters for
all the people
in your life*

> When I create with
> my heart, almost all of my original purpose
> remains. If it is with my head, hardly
> anything is left. One should not be afraid
> of being oneself, of expressing only oneself.
> If you are absolutely sincere, whatever you
> do or say will please others...
>
> MARC CHAGALL

Let me start off by saying that by nature, I am not a collector. Clutter tends to confuse me as does having too many clothes in my closet. I like to keep only what I use, and frequently go through my possessions to see what can be passed on. Having admitted that, I must confess that I have saved every love letter, card and note ever received from close friends and special intimates over these many years dating back to 1970. I have stored them in everything from old shoe boxes to sweater bags, and always make space for these treasured remembrances when I move. I've spoken with many other people and the consensus is that most of us save these words of endearment, encouragement and love.

So often in our daily encounters including telephone conversations, we dilute, disregard or superimpose our own meaning to what we have heard. You know the familiar expressions, tuning out, or selective listening. I know that when I am feeling unlovable or depressed, I am often unaware and unmoved by positive messages or favorable events. A nationally-televised declaration of universal love would not melt my defenses. We also shut down around powerful hurts and major transitions. When our self esteem is faltering or fragile, it is enormously beneficial to read our treasured notes affirming our goodness and worthiness. It helps us remember our inherent value and reclaim our own positive self image.

I save letters because they are important reminders and a way to chronicle the journey of your life. A friend I know calls them a written photograph for the memory. They bring back moments in wonderful relationships and remind me of beautiful times and shared intimacies. They illuminate strengths that people perceive in you, and unlike a conversation that ends quickly, you can take time to inhale, appreciate and savor each line. They are a way to learn from relationships that have not ended amicably, and help you see patterns in your behavior. They document the history of a friendship, a love affair, marriage or partnership.

Letters include all of the treasures that pass between generations. There are the notes of encouragement from a parent, letters we write to our children when they are far away, or when they are close by but it seems like the best form of communication. I have written letters to my children about our feelings during the divorce and other significant, emotional or difficult experiences faced. When they were born, I wrote each of them a letter describing how I felt during the pregnancy and at their birth. I have stored them in a safe place for them to read when they grow up and I am no longer here. This way they will know how cherished and valued they have always been.

Sometimes there are things in our past that seem too difficult to express out loud, but that we wish to share. Writing letters is a great way to let our secrets live in a safe place. While sharing her thoughts on the subject, a dear friend told me...

> One of the most wonderful treasures I
> have is a few letters that my mother and
> father wrote early in their relationship,
> which were full of love and enthusiasm.
> What I actually saw of their relationship
> was not that, so I feel so happy and
> relieved to know that they did have better
> times and that my birth came out of one
> of those times.

Speaking about her relationships and the letters she has saved over the years...

> I rarely ever look at these things, but I
> think sometime when I am old, it will be
> valuable to look through them to
> remember that my life was longer than it
> seemed.

Personally, I love to write letters and I love to receive them. I like choosing stationary and cards, buying favorite stamps, and using different colored pens, stickers and decorations. I love to encourage people, support them, and be there in a meaningful way during important moments. Letter writing has become a lost art. It is so rare for people to send handwritten letters anymore, especially with E-mail, computers, faxes and all of the latest technology. I would love to be an elf in the mailbox to see the joyful reaction of someone who has received a specially designed or handwritten card in a festively decorated envelope. What a delightful sight to behold!

Because we don't have experience or confidence to write, it can seem very intimidating to many of us. We don't feel we know how to express our feelings and have never been encouraged in our lives to do so. We hear the voice of the inner critic, usually in the form of an old English teacher, who convinced us that we could never do it right. So instead, we have relied on messages in cards to express it for us. Or, we simply have never tried.

If someone you loved sent you a card with a simple but sincere sentiment, such as, *You are my sweetheart, I love spending time with you*, or *You are a wonderful friend/companion/lover*, how would you feel? You wouldn't analyze it for

179

grammatical correctness or judge it for poetic prose. No, I think you would smile broadly, touch it to your heart and tuck it away to reread and appreciate.

Sometimes the simplest form of communication and encouragement can change everything. As I was writing this book, so much fear would arise for me. Then I would get a great note from a friend, take a deep breath and continue on my journey reinforced. So don't let yourself be intimidated by thoughts of writing. There are so many easy ways to begin.

THE INTIMIDATION FREE ZONE

A wife's belief that her husband is courageous, or a husband's belief that his wife is beautiful, to some extent creates that courage or beauty. These are not so much accurate perceptions as they are an ushering in by belief. What we acknowledge and reinforce in ourselves grows brighter, and what we ignore or don't see grows dim. In an experiment in elementary schools, a group of children was randomly chosen and identified as high achievers. When the teachers were given these children's names, they treated them as if they could not fail. And guess what, those children did in fact shine brightly, demonstrating their greatest potentials.

Wouldn't it be miraculous if we could let go of all of our past assumptions and recognize what we see demonstrated in someone now? I assure you that the more loving gestures you express, the more love will magnify in your life. A profound Yiddish proverb says, *My tailor is the only one who measures me anew each time we meet.* Give yourself and others permission to see people and situations from a fresh, new perspective, letting go of any preconceptions or prejudices.

THE FIRST STEP WITH LOVERS AND PARTNERS

If writing feelings is new to you, start collecting cards that have a beautiful picture or saying that you would like to convey. Then you have them readily available when you want to send the perfect card. Even though the card might have an expression already contained, write you own sentiment, no matter how short, before you sign your name. Your special someone wants to hear words from you, no matter how tentative your attempts might seem. How about something simple like *Thank you for sharing my life,* or *It feels wonderful to have you to come home to,* or *I'm glad we had a chance to talk things through, I feel very open and safe with you,* or *I love wrapping my arms around you and cuddling/making love,* or *Thank you for all of the ways that you love me.*

If you are having a hard time starting the message, think of all of the ways that you are together as friends and as a couple and then focus your sentiment on those experiences.

Here are the things people really want to hear from us in one form or another:

> ♥ *You are the most special man/woman in the world to me.*
> ♥ *I cherish and adore you.*
> ♥ *You are the best lover ever.*
> ♥ *You are beautiful to me.*
> ♥ *I appreciate you so much.*
> ♥ *Thank you for sharing you life with me.*
> ♥ *I really love being in a relationship with you.*
> ♥ *You are the most important treasure in my life.*

Obviously do not say something that is not true for you. But do find the sentiments that are true and express them liberally!

LOVE NOTES

Another easy way to express yourself is to write short notes. Use small notepads or those sticky notes and go wild. Let people know how you feel. Start tucking notes everywhere. You can put them up on the mirror as the first thing they will see in the morning, or you can tuck them in a sock drawer, a lunch box, on the coffeepot, in a briefcase, or on the car windshield.

Some suggestions would be:

- ♥ *I appreciate how you care about me.*
- ♥ *I love the thoughtful way you take care of my car.*
- ♥ *Thank you for always smiling when you see me and holding out your arms for a hug.*
- ♥ *Drive safely, you're precious.*
- ♥ *Thank you for choosing me to share your affection, love and life with.*
- ♥ *I loved making love with you.*
- ♥ *Thank you for breakfast this morning.*
- ♥ *Can't wait to see you at the end of the day.*
- ♥ *You're a treasure.*

There are a million ways to express yourself. Don't take any of them for granted. The more you acknowledge, the more the other person starts to see themselves in that way and becomes greater in their expression of it.

THE NEXT STEP

When you are more comfortable with your writing or expressing a few lines, venture out a bit. Now that your feet are wet, write your own letter.

Before you begin, you can jot down a few notes or things you want to be sure to express. Then you can start weaving the thoughts into sentences. Don't worry about grammar, punctuation or any of that at first. Just go at it in a free fall creative way without editing yourself. Feelings are much more alive and accessible if you are not censuring or worrying about how it looks. Write it all down on scrap paper. What are your favorite words that describe your partner? What are the qualities you want to praise? You can combine words differently for fun. How about...

- *a delicious personality*
- *recklessly beautiful*
- *wildly playful*
- *screamingly handsome*

Start off with a short letter and then you can get braver and make them longer. When you have your letter written, put it on beautiful note paper or a card and send it off in the arms of the letter carrier, or place it somewhere where it will be discovered.

LETTERS TO CHILDREN

I remember being in a workshop years ago where the facilitator asked us to write down three messages we wish we had been told when we were young. Our answers included *I love you unconditionally, I'm so glad you were born,* to *You are a unique and wonderful child and I love you just the way you are.* Then we played a game where we got to whisper all the messages to each other and hear them back repeatedly. It was a very powerful experience. Most people were moved to tears by what they heard and how it made them feel.

There are so many small, but significant, messages that you can give to children now that will bolster their confidence, give them a feeling of security and love, and expand their courage and willingness to risk because they know they are supported in life. How different our lives would be if the voices that spoke to us were the positive and encouraging ones instead of the critical and disapproving ones. If you have children, I highly recommend that you write them letters of appreciation, acknowledgment and affirmation.

Children especially love receiving mail and anticipate letter opening with great joy (they haven't gotten bills or junk mail yet!). It's so much fun to surprise them with a letter in the mailbox.

Send your child a letter or a note every once in a while to tell them how you feel—*What a great kid you are; I love being your mom/dad. You are so special and I love you so much.* Or if you have spent some special time together, *I loved going to the park with you today. Wasn't it wonderful to swing so high up in the clouds? I didn't even get dizzy when you pushed me. Playing with you is one of my favorite things. Can we make a date to do it again soon?*

ON THEIR CREATIONS

- ⊠ *I love the way you use such beautiful colors in your paintings. That purple tree is breathtaking. I love the way you open my eyes to see new colors in the world.*

- ⊠ *Your room looks great. I love the way you organize all of your special treasures. Maybe you could help me do the same in my room.*

- ⊠ *You are a great inventor! Look at all of those ingredients you thought to put together. I admire your style.*

NOTES OF ENCOURAGEMENT AND PRAISE

You can send a note of encouragement for the times that are disappointing too —

- ✒ *I'm sorry you didn't get the part you wanted in the play. You did a terrific job at the audition. You knew all of the lines and sung so beautifully. I know how hard you worked at it. You'll do a great job with the part you were given and I'll be in the front row cheering. I have so much admiration for you.*

185

> ✢ *Great job in your game today. You handled the ball so well. You have been practicing hard. I admire your perseverance.*

INVITATION SUGGESTIONS

You can also send an invitation to something you are planning to do together—

Come join me at the movies on Saturday.

Your Secret Friend

Bring the enclosed coupon for a popcorn and a drink.

It is often more challenging to relate verbally with adolescents, so note-writing and card giving create an ideal bridge to positive and regular communication. Send a card with a brief note that expresses a sentiment or aligns you with them in some way. Try inviting them out for a treat and some time together for just the two of you. It will mean the world to them.

LETTERS TO FAMILY, FRIENDS AND OTHERS

Sending letters to your parents, friends and relatives is a wonderful way for them to feel appreciated and valued. Remember to encourage them during challenging times and thank them for kindnesses offered. Clip an article they might like, or use the ideas suggested in the gift section of this book for sending inspirational thoughts and quotes. You can design and send them an invitation to see a movie, to go hiking in the woods or whatever activity you would like to share together.

WORD GAMES

This is a wonderful impromptu word gift that you can give to someone while you are on a car ride or just sitting around. Take out a pad of paper and start listing what is wonderful about the person that you are with. Just out of the blue—keep reeling them off.

1. *You are brave.*
2. *You are loving.*
3. *You have a great smile that lights me up.*
4. *You are incredibly affectionate.*
5. *You are a great friend.*
6. *You are a wonderful parent.*
7. *You are a delightful lover.*
8. *You have the best sense of humor.*
9. *You are a wonderful cook.*
10. *You are a great help mate.*
11. *You are a loving and courageous person.*

You can even speak them out loud as you are writing them down (certainly more meaningful and memorable than listening to talk radio). Then, give them the list to read, save and share. Usually what happens is that the other person will start describing the great qualities they see in you. Another wonderful idea is to make a list and leave it on someone's pillow. Wouldn't you like to find something like that on your pillow at the end of the day?

LOVE POEMS AND POETRY BOOKS

So many of us are inspired and moved by beautiful poetry. There are some wonderful books for your enjoyment. You can purchase them or borrow them from the library. Leisurely go through the poetry and reacquaint yourself with favorite poems as well as introducing yourself to new ones. Copy your favorites—the ones that really resonate with you or would speak to your partner. Write them out on a store bought card or handmake one using special paper. You can present them as a gift to a loved one, either in person or through the mail. Attach a note saying *This poem is so beautiful, it made me think of you*, or *This is one of my favorites and I wanted you to have it*, or *This poet expresses best what I feel for you.*

A lovely book that I recommend you own is *Passionate Love Letters, An Anthology of Desire* by Michelle Louric, published by Shooting Star Press. It has wonderful letters in it and is presented in a delightful way, including beautiful illustrations and envelopes with sample writing throughout.

Section

Six

Summing up...

When joy is elusive...
what to do when you're sad and blue

Joy can have a lot of faces. In our culture, we associate it with feelings of exuberance, delight and happiness that usually comes from things occurring in a way that is comfortable and peaceful, and has the spark that elevates it to one of life's great moments. When things are going our way, meaning according to our plans and assumptions, when we are not thrown off balance by too many curve balls, then we allow ourselves to be lulled into a place of security where we feel we have room to expand.

But it's an illusion.

I'm sure if we all looked back over our lives, we would have many great examples to dispel this myth of security. We have all had situations that seemed at the time to be our darkest moments that instead opened us up to a life-changing possibility. There have been times when we skated off into carefree oblivion, only to crash into barriers we had not anticipated. We have had times when we have despaired of the thing we were longing for most, ever occurring in our lives, only to find it peeking out at us from around the corner.

My favorite example of this is a friend, who on Thursday of a particular week, went into total despair of ever having the deep loving relationship she yearned for. Her partner showed up the next Sunday!

Nothing is as it seems to be. We have seen relationships we were certain of dissolve without warning or reason. We have also received spontaneous miracles where we were gifted in the most unexpected ways. I am a fierce believer in spirit

191

and in the *less visible* world of faith and trust. I believe we are all held and helped in ways we can't even imagine.

If the concept was shaky for me initially, writing this book has been a shining example of multiple miracles. Again and again I was shown that my perspective was limited and had nothing to do with the infinite grace and expanse of possibility that was abundantly available to me. My job, I found, is to remember to practice faith in every moment, to show up, be present and let go of my past assumptions about life. I think that we are all conditioned to believe that life, *if you do it right*, will be a somewhat smooth course with the occasional and unfortunate hurdles and bumps that you need to go through. Hopefully, not too many and not too long, before you would be back on course again. Or, we believe that life brings only insurmountable obstacles and that happiness and our heart's desires will always be elusive. Of course, experience shows us something quite different.

Life is a vast continuum and expanse of possibility, change, risk, growth, uncertainty, choice, as well as grace. Take a moment to feel how short our incarnation is here, and how precious our time together is regardless of what we are feeling in this particular moment. Our time with our children is short and fleeting. Before they are grown, we notice that our own bodies are aging, and before long parents and others we love are slipping away. We must all endure physical loss on every level, as well as the emotional challenges and fears we all face as human beings.

There needs to be a place where you surrender your idea of what life is, and understand that we all live with a very limited spectrum of understanding. The shakiness of the ground beneath us might, in fact, be the rumblings of a foundation for a much more brilliant or expansive reality. What we can do in any given moment of sorrow or fear, is to treat ourselves and others with compassion, tenderness and respect. We must find our happiness in our acceptance and our faith. We must feel our connection to whatever is Greater, however we name or identify that presence.

Learn to be present in love in whatever way you are able to. In honoring ourselves during those moments, we find a way to honor all of life. The *JOY* is in allowing ourselves to feel deeply, unresistant to life and change, where we stop bracing and protecting ourselves, and can open up to a greater wisdom and a Higher power. In this place, lies deep Heart-centered gratitude and integrity.

I try to remember this when I cannot seem to connect anywhere, or when I am so immersed in my own pain, that I cannot feel beyond my tears. I take time to walk in nature, to meditate, to commune quietly and to realize there will be unexplained loss and grief that only time and acceptance can heal. During these especially difficult periods, treat yourself with tender love and kindness, and live in faith. Learn to ask for help from those you trust. Remember that certainty is not part of the journey here.

Anne Frank said it best,

My advice is go outside enjoy nature and the sunshine and try to recapture the happiness in yourself and in God. Think of all of the beauty that is still left in you and around you, and be happy.

The Well-stocked Basic Essential Delight Pantry

If you want to have on hand the makings for impromptu delight, here is a good list of what to keep on hand. Just keep your eyes open as you go along in your travels for the following items that suit your taste and your particular fancy.

For letter writing and gifts...

- Greeting cards
- Blank stationary and note paper
- Sticky notes
- A nice writing instrument
- Stickers, colored markers and rubber stamps
- Blank labels
- Posterboard (for signs of all sorts)
- Clear cellophane and ribbon for gift wrapping
- Dime store paintbrushes
- Beautiful boxes, gift bags and tissue paper
- Glitter glue pens
- Gift tags
- Large pads of paper for brainstorming

BOOKS

- [ ] Books with inspirational quotes
- [ ] Poetry books
- [ ] Picture books of favorite places
- [ ] Good simple cookbooks
- [ ] Wonderful kids' books
- [ ] Limerick books
- [ ] Books with prayers or blessings you love

FOR THE BATH

- ♥ Bubble bath and oils

- ♥ Fragrant soaps
- ♥ Candles of all sorts
- ♥ Votive and other candleholders
- ♥ Matches
- ♥ Incense or aroma therapy
- ♥ A variety of massage oils
- ♥ Bath toys (rubber ducks) and wind up toys
- ♥ Loofah sponges, nail brushes
- ♥ Lovely thick towels

FOR THE KITCHEN

- ✕ A nice tablecloth
- ✕ A vase for flowers
- ✕ Teapot and assorted teas
- ✕ Bottles of wine or sparkling sodas or juices
- ✕ Assorted jams, jellies, sauces and spreads
- ✕ Empty spray bottles, jars and squeeze bottles
- ✕ Beautiful glasses
- ✕ Special mugs
- ✕ A tray with legs (for serving special treats)
- ✕ An array of candlestick holders and votive holders

GOOD TO HAVE ON HAND

- ☐ *Recipes for favorite dinners and desserts*
- ☐ *A file for favorite getaways, bed & breakfast and special romantic places*
- ☐ *Phone number of a good florist*
- ☐ *Phone numbers for meal delivery places*
- ☐ *Phone numbers for favorite restaurants, video stores, lingerie and gift shops*
- ☐ *Phone number of a great party store*
- ☐ *Phone numbers of best friends and your loved one's best friends*
- ☐ *Sizes and color preference for your partner's clothing and lingerie*

FUN TO HAVE ON HAND

- ♥ *Balloons*
- ♥ *A few small stuffed animals*
- ♥ *Little trinkets to include with an invitation*
- ♥ *Bubbles*
- ♥ *Small treats to add to a day, or an occasion, or as treats for your children*

Wonderful extras— accumulate as you can.

- ♥ *Fun costumes to wear*
- ♥ *Lingerie*
- ♥ *Polaroid camera and film*
- ♥ *Photo albums*
- ♥ *Heart-shaped soaps, chocolates and other assorted romantic goodies*
- ♥ *A nice scrapbook for all of your mementos*
- ♥ *Twinkly Christmas lights*
- ♥ *Assorted music for different settings adventures (Italian, French, Hawaiian, romantic)*
- ♥ *Small round table for two*

197

Be the Hero of your own Comic Book

W hen the journey of our life comes to a close, we will all have wished it to be a glorious adventure; one that was passionate and full, and where we dared to take more risks than we might have been comfortable with. A life inspired by our own gift of genius, that found a way to shine brilliantly in the world. In Deepak Chopra's book, *The Seven Spiritual Laws of Success*, the last law is the law of Dharma. Being in dharma is discovering the thing that you love, and finding a way to use that talent to serve humanity with love. It took me a long time and many courageous leaps to come back to that day on the grass in college when I emphatically knew my life's purpose was helping people feel more magic and possibility in life. My gift was evident as early as my childhood nickname of "Eloise," the irrepressible girl who wore toe shoes on her ears, had boundless creativity, and thought that *egg cups made very good hats*.

Find out what fills you with joy. Trust it, and pay attention to what your dreams, gifts and desires are. I hope that this book helps nurture you on your journey, by providing tools to live with more acknowledgment, praise, appreciation and courageous boldness. If you will commit to one small new gesture a week, and frame things a little differently for yourself and others, then you will notice magic happenings taking place in your world.

199

Be the hero of your own adventure here! Inside all of us is a wondrous woman and a superior man waiting to be born. Men might be from Mars and Women from Venus but our home together is here on Earth. So happy heroics and travels to each one of you as you make changes and choices for your lives. I would love it if you would write and share your stories, adventures, celebrations and new discoveries. I hold you in light, and am listening for a world with many more giggling adults!

Reasons that you'd want to turn this book into a

Number One
National
Bestseller

Everybody's talking about this book!
The intention of this book and of *A Sense of Delight* is to bring more joy into the world and into the heart of every being. How? Well obviously, the first way is to look at all of the individual choices we make in our lives and in the way we choose to travel thru the world each day. The next way is to get the word out about this book. I am creating a foundation where 10% of the profits of this book will be used to support more kindness in the world and to bring more delight to those that could really use it. Anyone who has an idea for something they would like to contribute, can write in and ask for a grant in the amounts of $100 to $1000. Maybe it would be to bring flowers to a nursing home on a weekly basis, or babysitting costs and a course for a single parent. Are there some children you know of who are aching to take a ballet class, or join a team and need some help with the costs. What about a great after school program that could be put together for latch-key kids. Why not take a person or a group of persons who are shut in, to a theatre performance and out to dinner? Being a huge fan of the outrageous, I'd clap enthusiastically to have someone pay 100

tolls at the toll booth and ask everyone who was waved through to pass on a kind gesture that day. I'd love to hear of someone handing out bouquets of flowers on the street to strangers who look like they could use a lift in spirits. How about a new wardrobe for someone getting back on their feet. Just write in and tell us your idea. I don't want the process to be intimidating; you're talking to someone who chose their college based on the ease of their application process (shhh!) but we do have a few guidelines and need a solid plan of how you are going to distribute the funds. Have fun with it. You can draw out your plan on your stomach with crayons and markers. No computer snobs here. If you enjoyed this book, let everyone know. (Haven't you ever dreamed of being an ambassador?) Why you can even call your local Congresspersons and while you have them on the phone, demand more time for bubble baths and less time in commuter traffic. If they have a hard time with that, just call your local bookstore instead, asking for this book and beseeching them to have me do a book signing. How many angels in full regalia do they get for book talks? I can guarantee they'll be delighted.

The more books that get out, the more money we have to share and the more work we can do, until all of us are bathed in the experience of 'way' more JOY!

Love to all ...

Marci.

> ...and don't forget to send all grant inquiries to:
> *A Sense of Delight,* 454 Las Gallinas, Suite 333, San Rafael, CA 94903

IF YOU'D LIKE TO ORDER MORE BOOKS, PLEASE USE THIS ORDER FORM.

Quantity	Cost per Copy		Total
1	A Sense of Delight		$ 15.00
2 or more	$14.50 each		$
3 or more	$12.00 each		$
	Subtotal		$
California residents, please add 7.25% sales tax			$
	Shipping/handling (1-3 books)		$ 3.00
	TOTAL ENCLOSED		$

Make checks payable and mail to:
A Sense of Delight
454 Las Gallinas
Suite 333
San Rafael, CA 94903

Please ship my books to:

NAME: _____

ADDRESS: _____

This book makes a great gift and can be autographed. How would you like the autograph to read?

_____

_____

_____

For Credit Card orders, call (800)852-4890.

PLEASE FEEL FREE TO MAKE COPIES OF THIS ORDER FORM.

GENUINE FAIRY DUST?
YES, PLEASE

Would you like your own little packet of fairy dust to sprinkle over yourself, your loved ones and to empower all your wishes and dreams?

Well, you are in luck because if you send us a self-addressed stamped envelope, two jokes and the lyrics to at least one Captain and Tennille song with $1.00 to cover our handling costs (you can't even get four large pieces of bubblegum for that, and besides all that develops then is cavities!), we will send you a packet of blessed fairy dust.

Mail your envelope to
A Sense of Delight
454 Las Gallinas
Suite 333
San Rafael, CA 94903

ABOUT THE AUTHOR

Nance Cheifetz has a Master's Degree in Education in Expressive Therapy. She is a writer, seminar leader, motivational speaker and, in her better moments, an angel (okay, that's a stretch!!!).

She does all of her lecturing in costume, with an eye towards delight. She is totally committed to creating more delight, kindness and humor in the world and in relationship.

She lives in Northern California and is available for bookings by contacting her at:

A Sense of Delight
454 Las Gallinas
Suite 333
San Rafael, CA 94903

Phone (415) 499-9161
Fax (415) 499-9161

Visit us on the web at www.senseofdelight.com or email to nancec@senseofdelight.com.